Leaving Laodicea

Table of Contents

2

Preface to the 2024 Edition

We've been through a lot in the last few years, and Laodicea's walls have been shaken. COVID, a wobbly economy, and natural disasters have all come to knock on the doors of our hearts. The real meaning of life got to peek through the mirage.

In the aftermath of COVID, we started hearing about the dangers of loneliness. Post hurricanes, we watched community in action. With a shaky economy, we're not feeling quite as confident of our paychecks as we once did. The pursuit of money seems a bit less likely to end in success.

That's where we are today. The knocking has been hard enough to cause a couple of pictures to drop off the walls and raise a cloud of dust.

But eventually the economy will heal. When the knocking stops, we can retreat into normal, rehang the pictures, and get back to being the good little Laodiceans we were before. We don't have to change.

We have started to see and hear about the value of community. But is it still something for "other people", or are we ready to start regenerating community in our own lives? Are we ready to orient our lives around something other than the pursuit of maximum material gain, and value the folks around us based on metrics other than the cars they drive?

The knocking is getting louder. Will we answer the call?

Introduction

What is Laodicea?

Revelation 3: 17-20a Because you say, "I am rich, and
have become wealthy, and have no need of anything,"
and you do not know that you are wretched, miserable,
poor, blind, and naked, I advise you to buy from Me gold
refined by fire so that you may become rich, and white
garments so that you may clothe yourself and the shame
of your nakedness will not be revealed; and eye salve to
apply to your eyes so that you may see. Those whom I
love, I rebuke and discipline; therefore be zealous
and repent. Behold, I stand at the door and knock...
(NASB)

Laodicea is a metaphor for a culture that defines being
rich as possessing "enough" material wealth. This idea
is what the modern Western world is built around. For
Laodiceans, riches don't come from family ties, from
doing work that brings you joy, or from the pursuit of
beauty. Those are extras, to be added to life when you
have a big enough pile of cash.

Laodicea is in the way we do business, the way we
choose friends, the way we shape our lives. Laodicea
can become almost physical in certain places, and is
much weaker in others, but this sense is due to the

numbers of Laodiceans in that locale, not the area itself.

Laodiceans hoard things and discard relationships. Our priorities are crystal clear when you look at our actions. We have made money our god, and its successful pursuit our arbiter of value.

"You think yourselves wealthy"

We look at our bank balances and piles of clothing and say, "I'm rich!" But our relationships are shallow things, based on circumstance. We network, but we don't put down roots.

We call ourselves rich, but when we grieve, when we rejoice, when hard times come, we find that our resources can't replace what we were told was "unimportant" and "not worth your time".

We believe that there will always be more – more money, more things. We believe that developing community can come "later". We believe that having families can come "later". These things are luxuries.

We put off childbearing later and later in life, we move away from our families of origin, we don't pursue friendships in adulthood, we don't belong to fraternal organizations and we're less involved in our churches.

Endless pursuit of money is life as we know it. The chase is how we value ourselves, value our neighbors, and choose our acquaintances. The first questions we ask on meeting another Laodicean surround the acquisition of money.

On the surface, Laodicea is rich indeed. We have access to more entertainment and luxury than our ancestors could have dreamt of. Machines do our chores, and we travel the world with less effort than our great grandparents travelled a hundred miles. We have less illness, lower infant mortality, longer lifespans – but there is something missing from our lives, from our souls.

In 2020, the world paused. The pandemic happened. This was our first knock on the door. The train of goods and services stuttered. The pursuit of money, power and fame skipped a beat. The inhabitants of Laodicea were forced to sit alone in their beautiful houses, alone with their piles of things.

Questions arose in the silence. Was this what we wanted from life? Were the luxuries what we wanted? Was it something different? Perhaps not – when we were forced to simply be with our stuff, we ended up spending our time cleaning out our homes and buying plants and dogs – buying connection. Forced to stop chasing after money and fame, we all had a moment to re-evaluate our lives. But do we want to keep going on the path of change – or do we want to go back to "normal", back to the cocoon of Laodicea?

Are we healthier, wiser, or more joyful because of our piles of stuff? We're starting to tear at one another, cancel one another, our fears blurring into anger. We are out of joint, out of spec. We are not living as we were intended to live, and we know this on a cellular level. We are broken.

The Biblical call to Laodicea was repentance; which simply means, "to turn around and go the other way". Isn't that what you do when you're on the wrong track – go somewhere else? Humans are resilient, we're problem solvers, we're able to do new things or old things in new ways. We have the knowledge we need, and we'll keep learning as we experiment.

We can't turn back the clock. History has lessons for us, not ready-made solutions. I want to learn from history and bring the best to the present while leaving the ugliness in the past.

I want to harness new technology and scientific observation for this project. We have so much knowledge at our fingertips. When we embrace the fact that we have a problem and solutions are possible, humans can get those solutions off the ground quickly and innovate.

The summons away from Laodicea seems impractical. How can we pay the mortgage and feed the cat if we exit the rat race? Are we going to be sidelined, missing opportunities? Are we going to harm our kids, chain down their dreams?

But life in Laodicea isn't great. Speaking only for myself, I hate crowds, I hate keeping up with the Joneses, and I want to make meaning and beauty.

I'm simultaneously lonely and overstimulated, constantly forced to interact with people I don't trust, and I don't spend nearly as much time with the people I love as I'd like. Do you feel like this too?

This book is going to try to convince you to leave Laodicea. That might mean leaving your city life – it might not. Laodicea, after all, is first and foremost a worldview, not a location.

If you do move somewhere Laodicea is less of the norm, this book will begin to equip you with the soft skills that you'll need to incorporate into a new community quickly. If you don't, it will equip you with another set of skills to change the place you live and encourage others to start sinking in deep roots and regenerate the community in which you live.

Why does this matter? Laodicea is a lie. We aren't rich without relationships. We can't value our pursuit of meaning by the number of zeroes in our bank balances. This lie is setting us up for hard times, and we are unprepared to do the things that we have to do to get through. The knocks on the door that we've all lived through in the last few years have shown us that Laodicea is just a mask.

When we embraced Laodicea as a culture, we ripped up the connections that form the basis of deep trust in one another. As we moved away from our families of origin in the 20th century and we've moved further away from each other, we see this poverty.

This movement was akin to the way that agribiz has exchanged long-term soil health for a few fat crops. Yes, it works – but it only works for a while. Then you look around and see soil depletion, or on the human front, you look around you and see relationship depletion. There's no one to cry with, no one to laugh with, no one to care.

Even in good times, humans and human connection are worth far more than gold – they're more important for our health, for our kids, for our parents... but we live in Laodicea, and we don't see what's in front of us. As that has started to change in a few places, we see the lack of connection, but we can't imagine a way back to societal health. Has it all gone too far? Are we doomed?

If I thought we were, I wouldn't write this book. It will take a lot of hard work and change – but I believe we can have lives richer than we ever dreamed.

If we leave Laodicea, if we sink our roots in and place value on things beyond dollar bills, we can be rich together. We can be rich in experiences, we can be rich in love, we can be rich in our connections. We can build something that outlasts us and something that will benefit our children and grandchildren.

Laodicea is full of glitter and glamour and ease. It's been crafted to appeal to our every desire. Leaving won't be easy. But it could save your life.

This book is for all who are tired of the rat race, of working hard and worrying about the future and feeling like they can't trust anyone. It's for all who are tired of taking momentary satisfaction in new toys and numbing themselves with new entertainments while they starve for meaningful work. It's for those who look at their cars, their screens, their lives and wonder, "is this all there is"?

How to Leave Laodicea

"Only you can find the courage to live meaningfully, at it is you who experiences the joy from doing so."
Marjolein Lips-Wiersma and Lani Morris [1]

The first step to leaving Laodicea is to take a hard, honest look at your life. Have you bought into the lie?

Look at where you are today. Examine carefully what you love, what you hate, and what you need to get by. Look at your dreams, what is it that you've always wanted from life.

Are you happy? How's your health? How are your relationships with your family? What kind of friendship network do you have – and how often do you participate in it? Are you satisfied with your search for meaning?

Leaving Laodicea isn't a one-size-fits-all prescription, it's a call to open the door to change. It's a call to walk in community. We all matter, we all can contribute,

[1] The Map of Meaningful Work (2e): A Practical Guide to Sustaining our Humanity by Marjolein Lips-Wiersma and Lani Morris, 2017

and we are all needed to break away and make a change.

Life isn't simple. But it is beautiful. Complicated and beautiful. You are more interesting than a machine, you have more potential, and you are infinitely more valuable. So are the people around you, your family, friends and neighbors. Leaving Laodicea means absorbing that truth and building your life around it.

We're going to have to re-value, and then re-form community, friendship, and family. Real community, with casseroles. Where one community takes hold and starts doing life together, loving each other, having each other's backs, more will follow. When we start making "community" mean something again, we'll see people wanting it. Someone must go first and become the light on the hill, someone must become the beacon to draw others home.

The next step is to examine the world around you for opportunities to change direction without starving the cat. Money **is** a useful tool – we just no longer wish to be its slaves. You might have more potential for change than you realize, if you think outside of the box. Where is the need? What are your talents? You don't have to participate in the rat race to win in life, especially when you redefine "winning" to align with what makes humans happy, healthy and whole.

The third step is to put heart and head together and make a commitment. If one's in and the other's out, you won't move a step. You have to want this. You have to be sick and tired of lies and frustrations and meaningless years slipping by like beads on a string. You must swear off false friendships, status symbols and empty laughter. You must get hungry for community, hungry for meaning, hungry for a better world, hungry for change.

This is our moment. We've been punched in the chest by the isolation and division of the past few years. We're feeling the pain of living in Laodicea. Some of us are looking for solutions to the pain. We don't need to "get back to normal" – we need to "work forward to healthy".

Life on earth is complicated. A simplified world can be broken down and used. Complicated people, living lives full of meaning, those people are harder to manipulate, more resilient. People living in community with rich relationships transcending external differences can cooperate to achieve goals that individuals can never conquer.

It's time to take a systems approach to life. No more smash and grab. Now it's time to participate and grow. No more using people because we need a solid professional network – now we participate in reciprocal, long-term community relationships. No more looking at one facet of a problem and running that into the ground, leaving further problems in its wake. Now we study the system itself in its most natural state and ask ourselves how to replicate and improve what nature put into place.

Inner cities could see a resurgence of health as small towns refill, if we all leave Laodicea together. We don't have to go back to farming – although more hands in the soil would be great. We can walk away from Laodicea wherever we stand in this moment.

And the last step – well, that's when you move on to a life so normal that you thought it only existed in a book.

Our lives can have the meaning and richness we've always craved, but to get it we can't pull ourselves apart – to get there from here, we have to dive in. We must live. Let us become complicated, passionate, beautiful and connected. Let us thrive.

Regeneration

"The ultimate goal of farming is not the growing of crops, but the cultivation and perfection of human beings." Masanobu Fukuoka

You're going to hear a lot about regenerative agriculture throughout this book. What do pastures have to do with communities? We've been told that both were broken beyond repair. We were told that the 20th century killed our soil and set us on an irredeemable path to chemicals. We were told that the 20th century killed our small towns and that the future is to be lived in anonymous pods in megacities.

If one can be restored, can't the other? We can save the world and save our families at the same time. Maybe that's worth doing... at least it's worth knowing about. It's not the only way, but it will be the way for some.

I started reading about fungal networks and root networks in the Hidden Life of Trees [2] and fell in love.

---

[2] The Hidden Life of Trees: What They Feel, How They Communicate—Discoveries from A Secret World (The Mysteries of Nature,1) by Peter Wohlleben

I immediately started trying to inoculate my soil with microorganisms. Those interconnections, both in the fungal network and the network of roots, all unseen, things that we don't see, don't take seriously, and then thoughtlessly destroy – what an amazing metaphor for how important our interconnections are as humans. We have held onto our understanding that roots are important for us – at least the big roots – but lost our understanding of how the finest of fibers and totally unrelated species play into the health of the visible tree.

When I read **Bowling Alone** [3]and **Social**[4], I was reading about the same set of networks, only those networks were between people. I saw how important our wider social connections (**Bowling Alone**) and our intimate friendships (**Social**) affected our everyday lives, our health, and our futures.

We didn't understand what we were cutting when we cut ourselves free of our networks of small towns, generational neighborhoods, and community institutions. All we've looked at is the success of those few who survived the endless process of transplanting, all we want is the perfectly straight urban tree.

If there's anything that sets my teeth on edge, it's the sight of a tree stuck in a concrete square out in the middle of a parking lot. You know it's got a short, ugly life ahead of it. It's cut apart from everything that

---

[3] Bowling Alone: The Collapse and Revival of American Community by Robert D. Putnam, 2000
[4] Social: Why Our Brains Are Wired to Connect by Matthew Lieberman, 2013

makes for a healthy tree. So it is with the person trying to do life all on their own. Admiration? Certainly. They're doing a hard thing. But it's not healthy for them, and it's not making their surroundings – their soil – healthy either.

Food production is a lot like that. I was born in the 70s and I grew up with the understanding that we had made an irreparable choice to embrace agribiz. Good or bad, we were stuck. We had to feed the world, and agribiz was the way it worked... right? Our only alternative was famine. I consider myself somewhat crunchy, and before a few years ago, I'd never heard of restorative agriculture or permaculture. Oh, I'd heard a couple of the big names, like Joel Salatin, but I didn't know that his crazy ideas were making a difference in more than his own backyard.

My eyes were opened when I saw a documentary[5] where the transformation of desert to forest occurred in only a few years' time under careful stewardship. Change can happen! And it can happen quickly. Why can't it happen for humans as well as for dirt?

We didn't understand what we were destroying when we plowed the land, planted monocrops, used chemicals... we were trying for a huge harvest of food. And we got it! That's the thing – especially at the beginning, we got exactly what we were looking for with these methods, and we didn't see the damage done along the way.

---

[5] Changing Paradigms | Regenerative Agriculture: a Solution to our Global Crisis? | Full Documentary
https://www.youtube.com/watch?v=V6m-XlPnqxI

It's the same thing when we put up factory towns and pulled as many people as possible to big cities. We were chasing efficiency. We told kids to move away from their parents, that their lives would be better far away from home. And they were... because so many hometowns died. What matter the long-term cost to families, to children, to elders? Broken hearts don't show up on balance books – especially when the damage comes decades later. The immediate benefit was real.

It's quite a transition, moving from what has worked so well for the last century and more to something new. You might have known somewhere in the back of your head that someone was doing things differently – where does all that grass-fed beef come from, after all? But to know that you can make a living from it, not just a hobby? That's news. The same thing goes for changing our way of living. We have to ask the question – can this thrive, can this work? And what happens if we don't try?

We see how variety in fields creates healthier crops and fewer parasites, how too if we noticed how variety in communities makes opportunities to hear all sides of an argument and go away still respecting our neighbors? We know that monocrops rip resources out of the earth, and we know that loneliness kills. This world is supposed to be complex, not simple. Simplifying looks good on paper – but not in real life.

Our communities are in disarray. Our families. Our children. Our elders. But once upon a time, that was true of our fields. I grew up when pelicans were rare because of DDT. Now I see them every time I go near the ocean. The story of restorative agriculture, though it has only just begun, gives me hope for what may be the story of restorative community.

Regenerative Community:

An intentionally rebuilt (or built from scratch) community that bases its creation on what we know to be true of human nature. This knowledge comes from an examination of history as well as work being done by social scientists.

In regenerative community, it is understood that we must participate in the life of those around us to maximize both our own health and happiness as well as the most positive outcomes for others in our communities. Variety is prized in regenerative community, even though it can make things less efficient. Complexity is prized, as real life is complex. Over-simplification is for machines, not living systems.

Community –

What it is &
What it does

Community What it is & What it does

Definitions

"Remember that you are more than skin and bones. You are one thousand stories of before. One thousand stories of potential. One thousand stories you have yet to see and know and feel and breathe. There's more to come. And it's something beautiful." - Victoria Erickson

Bonding Relationships:
A bonded relationship is one where you are closely bonded with the other person. It is a friendship, a mutual membership in a small group, an inner circle kind of relationship. As a metaphor, think of the bonded group facing inward towards each other. This is a relationship that necessarily excludes others, simply by the nature of its relationship. If I have a circle of close friends, and I met you at the grocery store last week, you are not included in that circle, even if I invite you to have tea with us. In less emotionally loaded terms, you are a part of my mentoring group or you are not. It is not that entry is barred, it is that there is a cost in time and effort for forming and maintaining these relationships.

Within a bonded group, one forms tightly knit relationships. These people are most likely to perform the tasks of a community – bringing casseroles, doing errands, helping out. It is these bonded relationships that one can count on to become what is called the social safety net. Who will take you to your chemo appointment? Someone else with whom you have a bonded relationship.

Bonded relationships have limitations – they aren't inclusive, they don't allow for exchange of fresh ideas and fresh people, and they don't reach across the aisle. They're great for getting small projects completed, but bonded relationships have a size limitation. Big projects often need to include more people than you can share the deepest parts of your life with, which brings us to bridging relationships.

Bridging Relationships:
Bridging relationships are where we network. "I know a guy". Bridging relationships are where we source materials and services. Bridging relationships are where we gather information and build trust across communities.

A bridging relationship is a relationship where you and the other party (or parties) form a bridge. Picture a line of people facing outward, holding hands. Each hand is a bridge. The people I go to the gym with regularly, the other moms I meet while in the school pickup line, the person who sits near me in my mega-church – these are bridges. The relationship bridges my inner circle and theirs.

These relationships aren't particularly tight relationships, and they're focused on the outsides, or

on work that has to be done. Without the context,
you're likely to lose the relationship. Your co-workers,
the people you know from taking your kid to soccer,
and the folks who work with you at the shelter are all
bridging relationships.

Notes on Relationship Categories:
Both categories of relationship are important. You
need bonded relationships to form community and to
perform as a social safety net. You need bridging
relationships to keep fresh air and sunlight in your life
and to pull in the people you need to access. Bridging
relationships connect groups who are bonded and help
us travel from bonded group to bonded group. They
provide an introduction. The way you build and spend
social capital differs from bridging to bonding, but
social capital is, regardless, the lubrication for either
connection.

Because bridging costs less time and can flow into
networking (which benefits the individual
immediately), it has become increasingly popular.
Bonded relationships like friendship have been
relegated to the sidelines, which has resulted in a
plague of adults starved for non-romantic
relationships.

There is nothing wrong with networking to further
one's circle of acquaintance and, more importantly,
one's circle of influence. But a circle of acquaintance is
not community.

Relationship Groupings:

Community:
A) A locale (e.g. town, neighborhood)
B) A group of people in your local area with whom you regularly interact. (e.g. church, neighborhood watch, farmer's market, etc).

Everyone within a community may or may not be in a bonded relationship, but bonded relationships make up a solid network within the community. Community means casseroles. Not literally, how many of us have had a casserole this month? But if you are asking yourself, "is it possible for me to pop over to this person's home or place of business with material aid in case of need at a moment's notice" and the answer is "no", you are not in community. You may, however, be in...

Association:
A group of people drawn together by common interest, regardless of location. This can be professional or personal. Gluten-free bakers of America, the Sewing Guild, your church's denominational conference members – or just a group of folks with a common interest who haven't bothered to name themselves really. These are bridging relationships.

Almost NONE of these groups call themselves "associations", they normally call themselves "communities" but while they sometimes pass the hat to offer monetary assistance in case of emergency, most of its members can't just show up with food, warm blankets, or offers of babysitting.

Companion/ally/comrade:
Someone with whom one has common ground, common goals, and a reasonably pleasant relationship.

This is now often referred to as "friend", because Americans are mad to call everyone "friends". We are all on first-name bases, we all hug, we all make semi-intimate small talk. This confusion is not helpful, because while a companion might show up with a casserole, a companion is not one with whom one mourns. They may be good folk (and there is no insult in being a companion, one can only maintain so many true friendships) but they are outside the circle. This is a bridging relationship.

Friends:
A friend is someone with whom one shares a restingplace of the heart. Common interests spark friendships, but friendship is a thing of the soul, not the mind. I share interests with many, but intimate friendship goes beyond occupation or life stage. Friendship is a much closer bond than is the common use in our cultural lingo. Friends are in bonded relationship.

Acquaintance:
Someone one knows by sight and name, of however many minutes or years. One need have no common denominators. Neither ally or opponent, they are an unknown. Bridging relationship.

Opponent:
Someone on the other side of a debate or issue. An opponent can be one's bosom friend, but opposition is anathema to companionship. Companionship can't hold the stormy water of debate.

Enemy:
Someone who is actively working towards the detriment of oneself, one's family, one's friends, one's country. A true enemy tends to be the reverse of a bonded relationship – to really get a good enmity going, you must know someone fairly well. Opponents don't become enemies until things get personal.

Family:
Relation by blood or marriage. This is a bonded relationship. Friends can rise to the status of family, but they cannot truly be considered 'family" until they are not merely interested in your own needs but are willing to shoulder some of your obligations. Would your "sister" take in your aged mother in your absence? If yes, then she is truly family, even if you share not a drop of common blood.

Notes:
In Laodicea, circles of friends, organizations, and networks are often called communities – and yet you can belong to all of them and no one will show up with potatoes au gratin when your mother dies.

Miscellaneous Concepts:

Social Capital:
This is the commodity by which social favors are called in. Example: If I go to your mom's house and fix her leaky faucet while you're on vacation, I have earned social capital with your family. It would be gauche for me to say, "I fixed your mom's faucet, so you need to feed my cats" and such a statement would immediately drain the social wallet dry (words to that effect are offensive in nearly every culture) but that's more-or-less how this operates.

The give and take of social capital is one of the primary ways in which a bridging relationship turns into a bonded relationship in adulthood. Humans like to earn social capital, so it is a wise beginning to ask for small favors or information. This leaves you slightly in the other person's debt, which you can then repay, gradually enriching both parties with the exchange.

Think of the exercise as sending little rootlets out towards one another – you both grow stronger as they intertwine and exchange nutrition for mutual benefit. Trees in forests do this – they share resources and news with one another. If one tree is attacked by a certain pest, it tells the other trees about the attack, and they produce chemicals to discourage that type of pest. Trees also share nutritional resources.

Small favors are one stage of social capital, big favors are another. They have the potential to go extraordinarily well – or really poorly. That's why it's important to have a solid foundation of rootlets.

Example: If I ask you, my neighbor and friend, to give my son his first job, and after settling in, he works hard and is an asset to your business, our relationship will be strengthened. I'll still owe you (it was a big ask/big risk) but it's a good debt. If my son slacks off and isn't worth a penny, our relationship is damaged, and I owe you a ton of social capital.

Social capital is often generational – you earn or spend social capital not just as an individual but as a member of a group. I did your family a favor, I did your community a favor, I did your association a favor – as a member of whatever type of group, you are now obligated to me. This is one of the costs of membership in any group. It is a cost that in healthy groups is well repaid, but it is a cost.

If the movement of social capital is all one way, people feel the pinch and they decide that living in community comes at too high a cost. Young adults moving into a new community often feel this, as they have the ability to help in easily measurable ways. If they aren't looking at the long-term impacts of their labor, or if their community is so shallowly rooted that there are unlikely to be long-term benefits because everyone will have moved away and forgotten their input, it is completely fair that they'd think community is a burden. It's also much easier to spray fertilizer on the fields that slowly build up soil fertility.

It's important to see that there are good reasons why people moved away from communities, because we can't rebuild them without counting the cost.

"...there's a sophistication and real progress that comes from taking what we know about biological systems and applying it." - Kristin Ohlson [6]

---

[6] The Soil Will Save Us: How Scientists, Farmers, and Foodies Are Healing the Soil to Save the Planet by Kristin Ohlson ; 2014

Community — _What it is & What it does_

Regenerative Community

All community involves "... *a norm of generalized reciprocity. I'll do this for you without expecting anything specific back from you, in the confident expectation that someone else will do something for me down the road.*" - Robert Putnam[7]

Because community is necessary to humans, we've slapped the label "community" on everything that involves more than two people at a time. We barely understand what the word means anymore.

Networking events are not community. They might be useful for your career, they might be great places to meet like-minded people to address an issue or come together to share resources, but they don't involve showing up with a casserole when your mama dies.

Online friendships can be very real, as friendship has always been a meeting of minds and spirits. But community requires presence, not simply affection. I've flown clear across the country to see my online

[7] Bowling Alone: The Collapse and Revival of American Community by Robert D. Putnam, 2000

friends. I love them, I trust them – but they can't help me if my mom passes or a storm floods my neighborhood. Friendship is incredibly valuable – but is not community.

Associations of people who pursue the same areas of study, who have the same difficulties, or who keep the same kinds of dogs are not communities. They're useful, and I belong to several. But they're not the same thing. If we want to build community, we must focus on that – not on friendship, not on networking, and not on anything else.

Our lives are filled with almost-communities. We work together, we hang out together, we play together. Ideally, at least. Humans need face time. We acquire information from body language, smell and other subtleties that are unavailable except in person. Presence is vital. The plague years were detrimental to our mental and physical health – we need each other more than we thought possible. We cannot ignore this as we choose a new direction.

So, what is community? A) A locale (e.g. town, neighborhood) B) A group of people in your local area with whom you regularly interact. (e.g. church, neighborhood watch, farmer's market, etc).

What differentiates regenerative community from regular community? Intention and a thorough understanding of what it means to truly be in "community" with others. In regenerative community, we realize that the last century did substantial damage to communities all over the West and that we can't snap our fingers and have them reform. We must intentionally rebuild communities, either in the places where we live now, or in new places. In regenerating community, we acknowledge that we can't just slap a few people together and hope for the best. We're going to have to put in some work. Instead of stewarding the land, to build or rebuild a regenerative community, we must learn to steward *people*.

The more we learn about the complex nature of human psyches and the natural realm, the more we should find ways to take this learning and put it into action. Laodicean rulers know how important community is, how important friendship is, how important meaningful work is – and then manipulate their citizens to chase material things instead. This benefits the rulers directly and keeps the populace dependent. Laodicea likes its trees in neat little concrete boxes.

Regenerative community shall learn from social science and take that study as seriously as a naturalist takes the movement of buffalo across the prairie. How did they learn that healthy grasslands result from birds following ruminants? Observation. How did they take this into managed landscapes? Active stewardship.

We must follow their lead. Let us look at healthy communities across history, across culture, and the pockets of true community that persist. Then we can take those lessons and put them into action. There will be experiments that don't go perfectly. That's fine – we're doing science here, and that means that some theories will be dropped, others will be refined. As long as we see progress to our goal of a healthy society, we're headed in the right direction.

We can also study what has gone terribly wrong – what led to the death of communities? Was it the press of history and the lure of money? Were there other factors? How have we found ourselves here, so fragmented, so alone? Which communities made it, and which didn't?

A good community should ground individuals, give them a touchstone, and embrace them. Some communities will become part of our everyday lives, like church groups and extended family who live in proximity. Other communities are a lighter touch on our everyday lives but extend our influence out further.

The level of commitment needed to join a community like a monastery or convent, where one gives up one's individual ideals to pursue the common goal, is unrealistic for most Westerners. Let's start with the basics – we want people to join us. We're trying to reestablish healthy norms of interpersonal behavior. Going too far will keep people out. Good people that would be greatly beneficial to our new communities, people that we need.

This is what's tripped up so many intentional communities of the past – they decide on a very tight rule, and that kind of tight rule may suit those individuals who volunteer for it, but rarely is it suited for their children or grandchildren. Of course we're going to have standards of community! But those standards should be that of a forest – we want to be healthy, good, wise, thriving individuals. Our generational communities are not going to be a cornfield, where each stalk of corn is much like the others.

Individualism:

How do we reconcile the Western ideals of individualism with the needs of community? Each tree in the forest grows – it searches for its needs and stretches its limbs. As it does so, it becomes more and more valuable for the community as a whole. Trees share their resources but follow their own paths. Think of a person in community – if the person develops their own gifts, their own talents, they become a stronger member of the community, with more to offer.

As trees mature, they offer fruit, shade, organic matter (aka leaves) and more to the forest around us. So too we humans should strive to grow wise, capable, and successful. If we are connected within community, if our roots are intertwined, if we are healthy in soul, it will be only natural that we will then feed our communities, feed our forests, and give back all that we have been given and more. We don't have to make ourselves one blade of grass in a savannah, we don't have to lose ourselves, our individuality. We can grow, stretch, be ourselves, and intertwine our roots and branches. The goals of the individual and the goals of the community should not be mutually exclusive.

Strong individuals make strong communities. Community does not require communism, it does not require that you subsume yourself in the matrix, but it does require that you set aside time and energy to pursue the good of the community and its members. However strong the individual is, if he holds himself apart, he is not a contributing member of the team. However strong the individual is, he cannot do everything himself.

A tree is meant to live in a forest, not in a square of dirt in the middle of a parking lot. Don't you get sad, seeing those trees in the tiny boxes of dirt, out in the middle of baking asphalt? You know they're miserable – and you know that in 10 years they'll be replaced. A life treated as just another expendable. So too is the individual who refuses to live with and for others. He or she is there, they make their mark, and then they are erased, hauled away for firewood. Replaced. In a forest, when a mature tree falls, it benefits others for generations.

Stewards:

Let us think of ourselves as stewards, those of us who take the first steps away from Laodicea and towards meaning. What must stewards do? We need to supply water, soil, and sunlight – aka fellowship, meaning, and income sources. We need places to live and things to do, room to grow, a place to grow roots. We don't need to tell people how to live; we need to give them opportunities to thrive.

We cannot simplify ourselves into an easy, one-size-fits-all answer. The permaculture garden in the desert and the food forest in Canada do not address the same problems, and they don't use the same solutions. Likewise, a regenerative community in inner-city New

York and a regenerative community in a small town in Nebraska are facing very different challenges and have disparate opportunities for growth.

We must collect as much information as possible, and we must share that information. In place of nature study, we can study history and anthropology. What worked, before we started fracturing ourselves? What drove people away? What things create community, and what situations send people packing?

We have history books and anthropology studies galore. We have modern social science studies and even medical experimentation. We have knowledge!

In order to turn that knowledge into power, we have to have the will. What can give us this will? For some, it is simply gaining access to the first bits of knowledge – finding out how important our connections are to our wellbeing. For others, it is the fear of what will happen to us if we fail to reconnect.

The lure of Laodicea isn't going anywhere fast – saving a catastrophe, this movement into regenerative community is going to take focus. We must love what we create, and we must allow it to give back to us and become part of us quickly, or we will walk away.

Variety:

Much of the recent fracture that led us to Laodicea was the reallocation of resources to towns and cities. If there are fewer jobs in your small town, and over the mountain there's a bustling factory city, where do the young people go? In other times, it was greed – taking land from farmers to grow more sheep[8]. Any time we treat a human as a commodity, something to be reduced to numbers and used for our own ends, we're headed to Laodicea. We must treat humans as the precious creations they are, and explore how they can contribute to everyone, including themselves. Each human is like a plant in a permaculture food forest. Each brings his or her own contribution.

Regenerative community observes that nearly everyone in a traditional society is given meaningful work and a share in community life. Variety is prized in regenerative community. Humans are valued in regenerative community, as is inclusion. Young or old, strong or weak, we are all part of this journey. We were created to need one another, and we should take joy in our interdependence.

Consider artists and entertainers – they're the brightly colored blooms in your garden. They draw in beneficial insects, helping to keep the producers in the garden heavy with fruit and clean of pests. They produce herbs for flavor and medicine, joy to the heart, and the occasional nasturtium sandwich.

A garden would be so dreary without flowers – and a community would be dreary without artists. Artists and entertainers help the communities that they live in by drawing in visitors from other communities to contribute income for everyone. They support their

---

[8] The Causes and Effects of the Irish Potato Famine; History in Charts, 2019 https://historyincharts.com/the-aftermath-of-the-irish-potato-famine

communities by providing beauty, togetherness, and laughter.

Teachers, pastors, priests, and coaches are the tap-root plants, drawing up minerals from deep in the soil. Often not very showy, they materially benefit the plants surrounding them by bringing up matters that would long stay buried. Nurses, doctors, caretakers of all kinds are the nitrogen-fixing plants. Without them, the whole ecosystem soon collapses – so many plants are heavy nitrogen feeders. Our caretakers feed all of us.

Every good garden has heavy-bearing trees. Those patriarchs of the garden use resources in plenty – and fill the shelves at home and at market. What of the vine layer? The annual vegetable garden? Would you want a life without blueberries, tomatoes, carrots or wine? Every person has their place, their purpose, and working together we create greater health for all of us. As we study plants and animals, we learn how they work together to create bounty. As we study humans, we see how we thrive – and how we fall.

This is what it is to be in regenerative community – it is intention, it is care, it is stewardship.

Community What it is & What it does

Purposes of Community

"[Our] fate depends on not only whether [we] study, stay off drugs, go to church, but also on whether my neighbors do these things". – Robert Putnam[9]

Community does the things for its members as a whole that each member struggles to do on their own. Community provides a safety net. Community provides fellow workers in a time of crisis. Community provides a place to share resources, physical and non-physical. In our garden, connections not only transfer and create resilience, they help aerate and feed the soil so that it becomes progressively easier for each member to grow and thrive.

Community connections create resilience. Think of a fishing net. Each rope is tied to another rope, and then again and again and again. With ropes no bigger 'round than my fingertip, the net can catch hundreds of fish in a single pull. Think of a soccer net. A ball kicked by an athlete in his prime is brought to a halt by a few strands of fiber. This is resilience, this is what

---

[9] Bowling Alone: The Collapse and Revival of American Community by Robert D. Putnam, 2000

working together looks like. In the garden, these networks can be made of rootlets – or even fungi.

A community can be small or large. The bonds of the community can be strong or weak. A strong community composed of strong individuals who have lifelong bonds to one another is going to be able to act (catch fish) and react (catch flying balls) better than a weak one – but either net is going to do a better job than a stick, no matter how much stronger the stick is than the fiber. I've seen small communities of weak people cope with hard times, harder than any one member could manage on their own.

Consider our fishing net. If I draw out one of the ropes, the whole is weakened but fine. That's life. People die, people move away one at a time. As long as equivalent numbers mature in the community and join, the community retains its strength. But what if many strands pull themselves from the net all at once, and those strands are not replaced? Community collapses. And that's what's happened over the course of the last few centuries. Were those communities providing all that their members needed? No. Were they always great places to live? Also, no. But they gave their members things that no community-in-name-only can replace.

As we consider regenerative community, we need to learn from the past, not replicate it. Just as regenerative agriculture doesn't copy medieval crop rotation, we don't want to copy a small town from the 1920s. There were problems in those systems. We must learn from them, we must apply modern methods and be realistic about where we are and what people need today.

One of the major challenges presented to community formation today is that we are constantly told that we can provide ourselves with the needs that a community provides without sacrificing our time. All we have to do is earn enough money and we can buy what we need. (As if the pursuit of extreme wealth is not time-consuming). If we have enough wealth, enough power, enough status, we needn't worry about the vagaries of fate. That only happens to the people who cannot arrange their lives properly. This is the Laodicean mirage.

This offers an illusion of permanent independence and autonomy. But is it true? For the very richest, the 1% of the 1% of the 1%, it is. And even they can't buy trust, as many have found out. I call this one of the great lies of Laodicea, "trusting in your wealth". It is an illusion for everyone except those very few who can buy their network. For the rest of us, it makes more sense to invest in reciprocal relationships that improve over time. And so, we become stewards of one another and of ourselves.

Community What it is & What it Does

Care of the Aged

"...the more integrated we are with our community, the less likely we are to experience colds, heart attacks, strokes, cancer, depression, and premature death of all sorts." – Robert Putnam[10]

One of the burdens of modern life is wondering what to do with your older relatives – or, if you are an elder, wondering how you're going to navigate through life. It hits all of us sooner or later. Many in my age group are in what's called the 'sandwich generation' – trying to cope with kids and parents who both need our help. Laodicea is not kind to those who can't help themselves, the rush to greatness isn't meant to slow down.

I used to work as the coordinator for the ride ministry at church – I would pick up the phone to call a little old lady, find out what she needed from a ride, and where she lived. The call should last five minutes, tops. But those calls never lasted five minutes. Sometimes I was on the phone for an hour. I'd pray,

---

[10] Bowling Alone: The Collapse and Revival of American Community by Robert D. Putnam, 2000

I'd listen, I'd mmhmm, and I'd get off the phone feeling crushed. The folks I'd call were all alone in life, and my friendly voice might be the only one they'd hear that day. I wasn't enough, their ride wasn't going to be enough – they needed more. They needed a community; one that valued them, one that saw them. "Yes, please", they'd say, "I'd love to go to church. Can the ride take me to any other church activities? I'd love to go to those too."

Sometimes this dependency happened by chance, sometimes by choice. I heard the stories about estranged children, children who had simply moved away, divorces, deaths... and ailments on top of ailments. Eyesight dims with time, reflexes slow. It becomes unsafe to drive. This happens to all of us. It is a common pain.

In Laodicea, we don't want to see that all of us are mortals, all of us have pains. Laodicea values independence over everything. This is why our elders are desperate to keep their drivers licenses long after they should stop driving. We treat those who are unable to travel freely like children. If you can't do for yourself, you are less-than.

The hardest part of my job was finding drivers willing to be consistent, to make relationship, to just go to church every Sunday and drop by an elderly lady's house on the way. There were a few, but only a few. It wasn't always this way, but we've grown more and more independent, more and more fierce in our freedom. We don't see each other. Maybe we protect our eyes because of our innate empathy?

If you hook me to an MRI machine and hurt my friend, I react[11]. It's a lot easier to not bond with that hurting person, it keeps you safe from their pain. But someday that person will be you. Someday, that person will be someone that you love. We all have needs. When we allow ourselves to see the needs, it's a short step to feeling the pressure to do something about them. When we allow ourselves to see the needs, it's a short step to realizing that those needs will apply to us someday.

And the little old people sit alone. Untouched, with all the damage that creates (hug your little old gentlemen – they are touch starved). Unspoken to. Disregarded. Left. Extreme old age is not a momentary stage, it can last for decades. Decades spent alone in a room, with no way to go farther than the mailbox. If you're not afraid of what this will do when it comes for you, consider those around you.

Our parents are aging, and gradually require more and more help. If said parents aren't in our vicinity, they might not be particularly forthcoming about the depth of their need for assistance, as Laodicean culture prizes independence and autonomy above all else. Even when they are in our vicinity, some parents will hide their decline. In fact, that's all too common – if we know that they're not able to be independent, we might take that blessing away from them.

---

[11] Social: Why Our Brains Are Wired to Connect by Matthew Lieberman, 2013

The idea that we are immortal, forever young, forever vital – it's a lie. It's propped up from every angle in the world we live in, but it is a lie. Bodies age. Laodicea fights this reality with everything it has. It's an embarrassment to experience normal aging. An imposition.

Laodicea holds up those who are incredibly physically fit at advanced ages as models. Again, with the 1% of the 1%. Everyone else, to whom accident and illness and simple decay has occurred? They failed. We deny the reality of death and simultaneously deny the reality of aging. It is as if in Laodicea we never age past 40.

In a fully functioning multi-generational community, those who age can receive help in small doses from a variety of sources. In exchange, they can teach skills and impart history, listen to the woes of those younger than them, and offer wisdom. In a fully functioning community, the needs of the aging can be spread across their whole family, neighbors, and friends, so no one has to do everything. This interaction benefits the elder, who is not left alone for days or weeks at a time. Nursing home care is left to the last possible moment, and instead of being left to sit alone, the elder is still visited and watched over until their last breath.

Elders are often thrilled to be included, but life in Laodicea has left many of them feeling less than valuable. A little diplomacy and the right person is what it takes to get them out of their houses and onto front porches telling the kids a story. These people-whisperers are among us, and can get Mr. Charles from, "oh those kids don't want to hear about my life" to telling stories about how he grew up in the course of a few visits.

Giving Mr. Charles a longer, healthier life is worth doing – and learning the lessons he has stored from a lifetime is worth getting. Reintegrating our elders is like having a master gardener visit your backyard garden. The benefits in knowledge will last for decades.

And it's not just direct benefit – consider the growth in empathy as all our generations learn to listen to one another again. There is a part of us that is used to sitting at our elders' feet and soaking in wisdom, and that part of us can be the first part to re-learn humility, charity, and patience.

Community — What it is & What it does

Children

"Social capital is especially important in keeping children from being born unhealthily small and in keeping teenagers from dropping out of school, hanging out on the streets, and having babies out of wedlock". – Robert Putnam[12]

Our elders aren't the only ones who need a village involved with their lives. As schools closed during the pandemic and parents were forced to find ways to keep their children safe and supervised while hoping to make a living, many of us had a cold dose of reality. We didn't have a backup system to take care of our kids and having their education snatched from them was a major problem.

We watched parents and school districts scramble to make do and in that scramble were revealed some of the most primal differences in wealth and poverty. Consider the outcomes for the children of the powerful and the children of the ordinary person through these years of hardship. Such emergencies are uncommon en masse, but very common in the particular –

---

[12] Bowling Alone: The Collapse and Revival of American Community by Robert D. Putnam, 2000

everyone goes through hard times. Another Laodicean lie is that a "properly" managed life[13] doesn't involve pain or difficulty.

Taking care of our children and educating them are where a trustworthy community network shows its value. It's also a wonderful place to start building community – necessity is an excellent motivator. You could join a homeschool coop, where you don't have to teach every day or every subject, and maybe you don't have the kids every day – which might allow you to work on that side-gig. Maybe you're so good at something that you can get the folks around you to pay you for it – are you the PE teacher? [14] You could share days of childcare with your kids' classmates so that you can get into the office. You could work from home or work flexible hours.... the more options you have, the richer you are.

For too long we've used government services as our safety net – but government services aren't flexible. They can't be, it's not the nature of the beast. Top-down solutions don't solve problems as they arise, they solve the problems you had two years ago. Bureaucracy is slow.

In regenerative community, we observe that humans require flexibility and the ability to take action in the

[13] A properly managed life = a life where you make enough money to cover every eventuality and keep you completely free of all entanglements, preferably while allowing enough free time to spend 10 hours per week on fitness.
[14] Homeschool moms consider the PE teacher valuable and this can be a paying job. You can even go through some charter schools and offer this as a service.

moment. How shall we steward this towards our goal of health?

Everyone's solution is going to look different. There have been pathbreakers here for generations – check out what they've come up with. Every cloud has a silver lining, including the pandemic. We have all seen that the education system is broken. The dissolution of the ideal of public school is a real problem today, but if we treat it as an opportunity, we could remember it as one of the best things to happen to our society. We saw the decay and we left it behind.

Intact communities provide a framework for children to grow up with a surrounding value system. Intact communities provide teenagers and young adults opportunities to spread their wings and learn life-lessons in a supportive environment. A community affects all of its members – if your neighbors' kids are doing well, your kids are likely to do well. Community doesn't just keep the small people from running wild in the street – it's a rich and complex interaction with humans, each one of whom brings value to the table.

Rich and complicated interactions are what our public schools offered in the past century. The system was designed to provide socialization for our children and certain defining moments of life, like prom. It provided the opportunity for participation in sports, in music, and increased their opportunities to meet new people. When we paused in-person schooling during the plague years, the crumbling of the cultural norms did great damage to our children. Our kids need educating, but they also need socialization. They need life-markers and common experiences.

Children are not miniature adults. It's too easy for those of us with a classical turn of mind to say, "Let them study Latin at home!" and ignore baseball games. If we're going to harvest past and future for our children, we need to collect neighborhoods full of children just as we embrace the library at our fingertips. Not every kid will want to study quietly in a library all day. Some are going to want to chase grunion after midnight and some of them are going to want to learn to fight fires. As we consider how to regenerate community, we need to give opportunities to trustworthy adults to offer their best to our children.

Hooking kids up to the internet all day is not the answer for most kids – and not a good answer for any of them. It's a crutch. Crutches are useful when you have a broken leg, but you don't design your life around using them. Humans need other humans.

Children aren't just learning how to read and what part of speech "frog" is – they're learning how to have conversations, how to read a room, how to play – take turns and do cartwheels... and they can't do that alone. Our children took a lot of damage from the plague years. It behooves us to take the lesson and change things for the better.

Research has determined that our sensitivity to social rejection is so central to our well-being that our brains treat rejection like pain[15]. We can't just say, "ignore the other people!" The kids socialize on Discord and whatever the latest social media is this week – but it's quasi-socialization at best. There are no microexpressions, no raised eyebrows to signal disapproval, just text and emojis. Is it any wonder they're socially backward and confused?

Children are our future – new human beings. New possibilities. New lives. And those lives require shepherding, teaching, mentoring, coaching and love. Yes, humans can be predatory, and we must all keep lines of communication open and eyes peeled to keep our precious ones safe as they grow up. Humans are dangerous – but only some of us are predators, and the best defense against predators is to join hands and create a safety net of protectors, large and small. More information, more fresh air, more circulation of people – that's how you defeat that dragon.

And in the meantime, the kids need the opportunities that additional humans create in their lives. They need to be taught math and they need to be taught how to prune a fruit tree. They need to be taught to write, and they need to learn good sportsmanship. They need to be challenged, and they need to know that if they walk by Mrs. Y's house, she'll smile and tell them that they're beautiful. The young humans among us need variety, far more variety than just a handful of people that they live with can provide.

---

[15] Social: Why Our Brains Are Wired to Connect by Matthew Lieberman, 2013

Kids need big brothers and goofy uncles and wise grandmothers – and they need more of them than they're related to. Teenagers need kids to look up to them and aunts to give them advice when it's too hard to talk to mom. Elders need the life and light that children bring, the strong back of the young, and the opportunity to share their wisdom.

We were not meant to live segregated by age.

Children are a great reason to start community programs. It's like the first tree you plant – one lemon tree does not a food forest make, but everyone likes lemons. Similarly, the easiest place to see the need for community involvement is when we're talking about children. We want our kids to have long-term friendships, we want them to have other adults in their lives (adults that we trust) to provide mentoring and perspective, we want them to have a great hill to sled down in the wintertime. Everyone likes kids. Projects 'for the kids' are an easy buy-in for adults and are a great "common problem" to work on together.

Community *What it is & What it does*

Safety & Emergency Assistance

"Similarly, one citizen differs from another, but the salvation of the community is the common business of them all". - Aristotle[16]

One of the functions of a community is to make living areas safer in both day-to-day and emergency situations. Living together in a group is safer than living alone but living near others with whom you are not in community is much less safe than living within a community.

Fire departments, police and even armed forces are groups of people working together to keep the community safe. In big cities, these have evolved to be full-time, paid positions; but many rural communities rely on volunteer fire departments, and every country calls a draft when they go to war. When our safety is the goal, we work together.

It doesn't always feel safe to work together, especially in the last few years. We've been taught to fear the folks around us, fear opinions that differ from ours,

---

[16] Politics, Book 3 Chp 4

fear different ways of doing life. Asking the man up the block if he can share his video footage with me because of an intruder in my front yard or telling the lady four houses down about some sketchy people that have been drifting through should be a no-brainer.

A community can function as a neighborhood watch – if you know the folks who live in your neighborhood, you know who doesn't. That means you can have eyes out when something doesn't feel right. A culture of eyes on things that don't fit is a culture where it's safer to walk after dark.

If you feel some tie or obligation to the folks who live near you, when you notice something going down in or around their homes that is fishy, you can drift over and see if you can't be of service (or just alert the authorities). If you're in community with your neighbors, this doesn't feel intrusive and weird, it feels normal and safe.

But what if you live in a neighborhood where no one is in community, you just all live there? The crime rate will go up – no one will know who "that guy" is, so no one will call if they see him outside your front door. If you did call and were wrong, because you don't have a relationship, the call would be seen as an insult, not an honest mistake. What if someone becomes sick or injured? If you haven't seen Mrs. Mulgrew and you know her, you're a lot more likely to make it over to knock on the door and check on her than if you barely know her name. That could save Mrs. Mulgrew's life or yours.

Even though my neighborhood is not particularly tightly knit, it is still considered completely acceptable to share safety data, like camera footage. I've had neighbors knock on my door to say something odd happened and ask if I have any record of it. This, in fact, might be one way to start a relationship. "Hey, thanks for checking your cameras for me – I baked these cookies for you".

Emergency assistance is enhanced by cooperation. If your neighborhood can't be accessed because of weather conditions, it's better to share resources than go it alone. In an emergency a neighbor can lend a hand or a crowbar to load someone into a car or pull them out of a hole. But first one must know who might have a crowbar, know how to use it, and be trusted in your own home. We all have to work together in a crisis – but imagine how much easier it would be when the crisis came if we'd known each other and worked together beforehand.

This community help goes beyond neighborhoods. Your church community can band together in case of emergency and be a hub for resource sharing, a place to come together and assess needs and abilities quickly. Good churches within a neighborhood become beacons of safety and stability. Churches have a lot of practice in organizing people and resources – they already know who is gifted at keeping the ducks in rows.

Any fraternal organization that meets regularly and takes on tasks together can be a benefit in a time of need. They already have the connections and can move more quickly in a crisis than those who haven't had practice working together. Just another reason to grow connections now – but if the need comes before the net is built, this is where to start looking.

Community What it is & What it does

Community Culture

"Dying societies accumulate laws like dying men accumulate remedies" – Nicolas Gomez Davila

A facet of community that we try to avoid talking about is the creation and maintenance of community standards. "Folks around here do things this way". It reminds all of us of HOAs and the costs associated with living in small towns. No one wants to be controlled by the city fathers or become the subject of the city mothers' gossip circle. At the same time, wouldn't it be incredibly restful to finally feel as if you were doing life "right"?

It *is* desirable to live in a neighborhood with its own character, a town known for a certain something, to have some idea of 'what we're about'. There's a fine distinction between encouraging a vibe and being controlled. The difference is the willingness we have to come there in the first place, the enjoyment we take in the others who live there, whether we allow their choices to inspire us or if we, instead, feel dictated to.

The best way to avoid feeling controlled is to focus on two things: inspiration rather than orders and internal changes rather than external allegiance. If your neighborhood is known for forming relationships and an ethic of kindness, it's very difficult to drum up a proper rebellion. If your neighborhood is known to be a great place for kids to grow up, and adults are expected to keep a weather eye out for the kiddos and smile at their shenanigans, that too is something that is easily participated in.

If your neighborhood is noted for having identical shrubbery, it's quickly going to get at least boring if not annoying – "is that all you care about, my outsides?" That kind of rule makes people feel excluded and judged. Even the habit of wearing particularly nice hats (although fun) can get out of hand. This is where regenerative community comes in, not just a return to the past.

Let's spend some time learning our neighbor's hearts and lives and lift them up. We can't be about the outsides any longer, we must be about cheering each other on and loving each other with agape love. Everyone has a place in this world – let's help each other (and ourselves) find the right place to be so that we can all grow and thrive.

As we form community bonds, we will, without seeking it, also develop community standards. We will be wise to keep these standards inclusive, internal, and positive. We want to bring people in, hold people up, and help people to grow and thrive. If we foster health for the individuals in our communities, the communities themselves will grow stronger and healthier. Let's recognize that developing a community culture will happen as we develop community. What fruit do we want to be known for? We can begin as we mean to go on and make intentional choices from the get-go.

Community

What it is & What it does

Personal Meditations

This is where you start to build your "why". Here are some questions to ask yourself:

1) What parts of community most appeal to you? What would you love to see built around you?
2) How would regenerative community make your life richer, better, and easier?
3) What parts of community make you want to pull away? What's your disincentive to make this change?
4) How would a commitment to regenerative community make your life harder?
5) What do you think of the communities around you now?
6) Imagine yourself a steward of the people and networks around you. How can you imagine them pulling together to benefit everyone?
7) What needs that community supplies would you add to this list? (I definitely didn't hit everything).
8) What shadows of true community do you belong to now?

9) What real communities (aka church, healthy neighborhoods, etc) do you belong to now?
10) How are you handling the stewardship of your kids, parents, safety, etc. right now? Is it working for you? What do you see coming down the pike?

This chapter is only a beginning. As you allow yourself to contemplate what regenerative community might bring to your life, you're going to have a lot more to add. And once you start living it, you'll find even more.

Human Needs

Human Needs

A Dog Named Desire

"It is heart-rending to see people who have no respect for themselves and are unaware of any light or beauty in their lives. We have a sacred responsibility to encourage and illuminate all that is inherently good and special in each other." - John O'Donohue [17]

Laodiceans treat desire like a dog. We throw it a biscuit to stop its barking or lock it away where it can't be a bother, or we counterproductively over-indulge it. As we search for our way home, our way to rich, meaningful, interconnected lives, we must take a real look at our desires.

Poor dog. We assume that its barking is just noise, not a message, and if we look for meaning at all, we snatch at the first interpretation that the surrounding culture offers and use that. After all, we only want desire to be quiet.

We show off our desires like dogs in a competition. What else is a vision board than an attempt at harnessing the power of desire? Ah, but only the dogs who look most like the breed standard are welcome

---

[17] 17 Beauty: The Invisible Embrace by John O'Donohue, 2005

there – and likewise only desires that are some version of what everyone else is asking for are welcome in public discourse. Even our dreams are constrained.

We're constantly told what to want. What else is an influencer, but someone who influences your desires? Take travel as an example. Do you want to see the Mona Lisa in the Louvre? Do you want to know every landmark in your hometown, the county you grew up in? Do you want to be the one that knows the lore of Middle Earth – or of Middleton?[18]

One cannot accept the definitions of desire created by others. Your neighbors cannot tell you what your desire is screaming for, it is you that must take the time to sit down and listen. It's your dog.

When we're trying to figure out what that barking means, we start by putting the cards on the table of need. Food/shelter/transportation. Love. Maslow's hierarchy of needs might be helpful here if you need assistance in thinking this through. The trick is getting to the truth – not what the world tells you. It might take a bit to sort this out. That's time well spent.

If you don't get to the root of your desire, the craving behind the scream, the desire will not be satisfied. Your efforts, your time, your money, your heartache, they will all be in vain. Just a biscuit, thrown to a hungry dog who was asking for its supper and a bit of

---

[18] There is no reason for this to be "or" except that I want you to consider the never-mentioned alternatives to the dominant narrative. Feel free to make this "both".

affection. The dog will start barking again in a moment.

Finding your underlying hunger is work. But it is worthwhile. Once you know yourself and what you really want, you can pursue total satisfaction.

Reading Your Hunger

"The force for life should spring from the reality of who we are." - Jean Vanier[19]

Let us invite the hungers of three different people to sit down, unwind, and tell us what's on their hearts. The barking sounds to each person like, "we need to go to a popular theme park!" Very well. Let's keep listening and see what the rest of the story is...

B: "When Betty and her husband came back from [theme park], it was all they could talk about for months. The pictures were all over their social media. Her kids had such a good time, and my kids have asked me about this every day for the last six months. I just must make this happen!"

Y: "It's been a long year. I do the same things day in and day out. I deserve a break. I want to get out of here – I want to get out of reality. I feel like Dorothy in Kansas, everything is black and white and I'm starving for color".

---

[19] Community and Growth by Jean Vanier, 1989

Z: "I've always wanted to visit that state. While we're at [the theme park], I want to see [...] and I love a good road trip. It will be so awesome to show the kids the country as we drive to and from [theme park]. We're going to make so many memories!"

Three people all end up in the same culturally sanctioned space, but are they looking for the same thing? B wants to impress others and please her children. This is a checkmark to check, pictures to take, an indicator that she's of a certain income and likes the same things that her friends like. Y wants to get away from where she is. There is something seriously missing in her day-to-day life, and she's putting all her hopes for stimulation and/or respite into her trip to that park. Z is hungry for adventure. She doesn't want to just go to the park and ride rides with a character, she wants to make a trip out of it. The journey is greater than the destination.

The theme park itself is neutral. But if all three hungers just go to the park, they won't be satisfied. B does not want to drive cross country and stop at the world's biggest ball of twine. Z does not want to get on an airplane to land at the in-park hotel. Y doesn't want to come home... If we put them with the same travel agent, the same itinerary, based only on what they said in the first gasp, they'd all leave somewhat annoyed. B is still going to be in competition with her neighbors, Y is still going to hate the daily grind, and Z is still going to want more time on the open road.

If we want to satisfy the hunger, we must look at the hunger. And so seldom is hunger a one-stop-shop.

Humans are complex creatures, but we complicate simple things - sometimes so we don't have to see what lies behind the façade. Clear your mind and look at your desires – what are they on the surface, and what do those desires tell you about your deeper needs?

Human Needs

Redefining Wealth

"Radical Homemakers gauge their "wealth" by their ability to include in their lives such incalculable values as good relationships, good food, or self-determination. But equally powerful in their sense of fortune is their ability to determine what they can exclude." - Shannon Hayes [20]

Humans need basic physiological things. Food, clothing, sleep. We need safety, freedom from fear. We need acceptance and love. We need to improve ourselves and the world around us. We hunger to create. We want community and self-reliance. We want responsibility and freedom. We want love and truth, music and a sense of wonder. We want meaning, self-respect, and a deep relationship with those around us and the earth beneath our feet. We want to leave things better than when we arrived. We want, in short, for our lives to matter.

Instead of pursuing a life of meaning, too often we accept our culture's offering of the box entitled, "Wealth". Money can be a proxy for many things, but

---

[20] Radical Homemakers: Reclaiming Domesticity from a Consumer Culture by Shannon Hayes, 2010

the three main branches of its promises can be broken out into three classes: security, freedom, and status. Is that what it means to be wealthy – to you?

Security is a roof over your head, food in your belly, a neighborhood that you can walk through at night unharmed, and a general feeling of well-being. If you know that this is what you hunger for, when you climb up that corporate ladder, the first thing you might want to do is relocate to a 'better neighborhood' or put money into your savings account.

Money is a quick way to security. However, you need not bow to Mammon to get it – community can provide a safety net of other humans. Old neighborhoods in poor urban areas have been known to watch out for one another and provide some measure of security through solidarity. This requires that one not only invests substantially in social capital but that you find a network of others willing to do the same.

Freedom is the ability to do anything, go anywhere, say anything and not be tied down. It's shocking how many people will tie themselves to the wheel to buy the ability to be free. There are enough vocations in this world that require a spirit that loves walking on tightropes, a person ought not to have to spend years of time purchasing a few breaths of air. Are we making wise decisions? Yes, it costs money to travel to Xanadu, and yes, travel can be a proxy for freedom, but it's a poor exchange if you come home unchanged.

The third thing that money can buy is status. Designer clothes, expensive cars, the right parties with the right people, involvement in the right fads. It's all a show designed to prove your worth, a show that has no end. Because purchasing meaning through a show of status requires you to climb on the treadmill of endlessly impressing others who are on their own treadmills attempting to endlessly impress you.

If you're seeking meaning, fame is a poor proxy indeed. Instead, ask yourself – whose opinions matter to me? Why? What hunger does that desire cover? If it is a desire to make a difference, then attack that. If it is the very human desire to be known, this can be achieved more easily – and more satisfactorily – in a small group than in a large one.

Wealth is more than just numbers. Health is wealth. A life filled with art. Friendships. Family. A life of meaning and purpose. Our desires change as we age, as we go through the different seasons of our lives, but our characters don't change – and so the deepest things, the deepest hungers, hold steady.

Would a life, perfectly secure, full of long vacations to far-away places, be called "wealthy" if that life never had belly-laughs, never had a group of friends that you could cry with, never included the smell of a baby's head, never included the ache of muscles well-used after a long day working hard? If you didn't have people you could trust or starry skies overhead or a bird's song... would that life be called "wealthy"?

Not for me. I don't know about you – but I do know that you'll never achieve wealth until you define it. You might be within touching distance and never noticed it – because you never look up from chasing the willow-wisp. Laodicea is full of willow-wisps, do you want to chase them forever?

Learn who you are, what's important to you and chase that thing. It might be that you can build a life that fills your soul, your belly, and your community – and enjoy it while you live it. I'd like to see that – a world full of wealthy people, souls full and hearts overflowing with laughter.

Fame

"The desire for a feeling of importance is one of the chief distinguishing differences between mankind and the animals." - Dale Carnegie [21]

Fame, in and of itself, does not make you happy. For evidence, I present to you the biography section of the library. Fame is valuable – it is a medium of power, of influence. Fame can get you things. But fame has its price. A lack of privacy combined with loneliness, expectations from strangers, difficulty with trust (and thus friendship), as well as endless gossip only begin the list. Yet Laodicea tells us that only the famous "matter". They are the ones who make their mark on the world, and us lunks? We're meaningless, good only as fodder for the great ones.

We need the ones who fly. They inspire us, they change the direction of the world, they burst through boundaries as if they didn't exist. Most of us do not come with the burning in the belly that fuels the comet people. We desire meaningful work, human

---

[21] How to Win Friends and Influence People by Dale Carnegie, 1936

connection, children, and a place in our communities. We desire earned respect. We are grounded.

Those who fly like comets across the sky are not powered by ordinary desire. Mozart did not write his first symphony at eight years old because he thought that the piano might be interesting. He burned. Edison did not collect more than 500 patents because it was a hobby.

The originals, the leaders in their fields, they were consumed by their need to do, create, invent, explore, conquer, climb... they would have done these things for nothing, and to be honest, they frequently did. In so doing, they sacrificed the ordinary lives that bring satisfaction and joy to most folks. To fly, they cut loose the ties that bound them to the earth.

Laodicea has supplied us with endless lights in the sky to stare at, both real and faux. Without community, we don't know about the men and women who are living lives filled with profound meaning and happiness. That's why it's so easy to write ourselves off as nothings. We have no examples. Without community, we have no reason to look across the street for success, we only look up. In looking up, we compare ourselves to the ones who cannot sleep at night for the intensity of their dreams, and we come up lacking. Not all of us are made so – and if we all were, we'd run out of bread and safe streets quickly. It is good to have variety. The comets are good, and it is good that they are few.

It is not that we do not want – and need – achievement. We need meaning, and meaningful work. We very much do. But we do not know the names of artists and craftspeople who are leaders in their fields, who live lives full of joy. We don't know mothers or bakers or plumbers; we only know the famous. And so, we all strive to be famous.

Those who were created to be comets have always been and will always be part of our world, and they will change the course of history. Those who seek to emulate them without the burning in the belly burn to ash.

Fame is one of the things that we are told to pursue, at whatever cost to ourselves and our loved ones. To be famous is to be seen, to be praised – it is to reflect light on the ones who "knew you when". We enjoy watching the famous, we enjoy daydreaming about them.

We gossip about their private lives, we envy their possessions, we sigh at their accomplishments, we strategize over their methodology, desperate to reproduce their success... and yet, they are strangers. The famous might as well be fish in an aquarium. They're captives, their lives lived for our amusement.

The pursuit of fame is an endless effort to gather enough fuel and get enough flame to claim a place. We don't look at the cost of fame to the famous, we don't look at their lives and ask if they are happy. We just want to be known. Comets can't be stopped; they are forces of nature. If you are one of those forces,

Godspeed. Most of us, however, are meant to build history by stewarding the people and communities around us. We're meant to change the world one step at a time. This is a good thing, and a beautiful one.

When we leave Laodicea, we choose to be known and know in return, to be a part of a community. Our lives will matter to those who can see our faces and touch our hands. This in turn will enrich our lives and the lives of our families. We invest in people and are repaid, and this investment pays off over the course of generations.

Human Needs

The Desire for Stewardship

"Money is not the only commodity that is fun to give. We can give time, we can give our expertise, we can give our love or simply give a smile. What does that cost? The point is, none of us can ever run out of something worthwhile to give." — Steve Goodier

Laodicea likes to tell us that our basest, most selfish desires are the most real. To find ourselves is to give into those desires, to admit them, to live them. But what if that endless cacophony of barking was code for the selfless desires we've never even explored? Stop. Look. Listen. When you give into your basest desires, how long does satisfaction last?

We all want to be good stewards. Funny that, how our deepest hearts cry out for what we were originally commanded to do. "But", you say, "humans are intrinsically selfish creatures". Yes, we are. But we hate that about ourselves, and that internal dichotomy, the tension between our base desires and the pull of our hearts, is one of the tells that we are meant for more.

Stewardship – that sounds like a money thing, doesn't it? That's how we use it in our culture, to the near-total exclusion of anything else. And it is a money thing. But it is not ONLY a money thing. Stewardship is the action of taking what we have been given and using it well, with a mind for those who come after us, and the One who gave it in the first place.

What have you been given? The desire in your heart – that need to do. The assets in your environment, not only in your bank account but in your time, your social network, your health, your freedoms, your opportunities. The talents that have blossomed over the years. The skills gained. These are what you have stewardship over.

You are not a steward of what you have not been given authority over. I am not a steward of Mount Everest's litter problem, although it annoys me. How not? Well, I'm not a mountain climber, I don't live in Nepal, I don't sell hiking supplies... there's no part of my life that intersects with that issue. Now, if you want to talk about drug addiction and homelessness? Err. I do live in a largish city in Southern California, so that's real life. How about the emptiness of modern interpersonal interaction (again, I live in a military town in Southern California...)? Oh. Now, that's my problem.

There will be pressure to not explore your desire for stewardship. You will be told that it's not possible; or if possible, not reasonable; or if reasonable, not sensible. Not everyone is called to be Mother Teresa, but everyone does want to be someone. And everyone can be someone. You steward that which you have been given, nothing else is required of you – and nothing less is expected of you. The expectations of stewardship keep me up at night and give me my greatest joys.

Michelangelo contributed to the world. So did the one who taught him to paint and the one who built his scaffold. And where would you be without that teacher, coach, neighbor, friend who spoke into your life at just the right moment? Significance is more easily obtainable when you set your eyes to stewardship.

Human Needs

Meaningful Work

"[The four paths to meaningful work are] Integrity with Self, Unity with Others; Service to Others and Expressing Full Potential". - Marjolein Lips-Wiersma and Lani Morris [22]

We want meaningful work. But what does "meaningful work" mean? Work with meaning – it doesn't mean just work that matters to society. It means work that matters to the individual. During the pandemic, a lot of us got a chance to take time off and think about whether what we spent our days doing really mattered – and lots of us decided that it didn't. After the lockdowns came the Great Resignation. Folks changed jobs, retired, shifted employment at a historic rate. Our actions answered the question – whatever it was that we were doing, it didn't fill that void.

We've been automatons so long that when we were let out of our boxes it's like we encountered a whole new world. In this world we all developed a deep interest in keeping sourdough starter, taking walks outdoors, and buying dogs. But most of us aren't going to open

[22] The Map of Meaningful Work (2e): A Practical Guide to Sustaining our Humanity by Marjolein Lips-Wiersma and Lani Morris, 2017

bakeries now that we have to go back to work, and while pet sitting and dog walking are probably about to be a boom industry, there's not enough room for all of us. What then?

Creators need to make things. A garden, a garment, a community, a song, a chocolate cake - they must create. We see creators not just building roads, but creating systems, not just writing sonnets but building bridges.

Fixers see beauty in old things, and they long to make them new again. That could be a piece of furniture, a car, a downtown area ravaged by poverty. Never happier than when they're pottering in the garden or the tool shed, this person brings new life where decay has set in.

Healers, hearts ever open to another's pain, have hands that look for ways to show love in a concrete fashion. Doctor, nurse, psychiatrist – those are job titles. You might find a healer looking to repair the soil, a relationship, a body, or a community.

Seekers look for truth. They collect knowledge the way a creator might collect fabric scraps, and they give it out. Their passion is the light of discovery and the understanding on a face when that knowledge is transmitted. They're also sometimes called explorers, and you can find them equally mapping uncharted territory and in the corridors of academe.

Protectors put their bodies and their skills to work keeping their communities, their families, their countries, and/or their values from harm. First into the fray, the warrior spirit finds satisfaction in creating safety for others. This spirit is found equally in the lookout crying out warnings and the one who leaps to respond to that call.

Most of us have more than one of those desires inborn in our hearts. You have been fearfully and wonderfully made. You have been given a desire which you alone are best suited to pursue, and in the pursuit of which you will find life's greatest satisfaction.

And Laodicea tells you that you'd rather have a Ferrari! We are all constantly told that we **want** to be selfish, when the opposite is true. Our truest selves hate our selfish, transitory, desires, hate them even while we give into them, hate them when we embrace them and identify ourselves with them. No – we don't want to be selfish; we want to be good stewards! Certainly, we all want our needs met, but that's not all of who we are.

We want to make a positive difference in the world, we want to know on our deathbeds that the world is a better place for what we have done with our lives.

What form that difference takes, what number of people it affects, whether it's a hobby or a career, an avocation or a commitment to being available, that varies. The constant is that we want our lives to make the world a richer place.

Human Needs

Participation

"A meaningful life is a responsible life and we need to be able to stay in charge of what makes life meaningful for us." - Marjolein Lips-Wiersma and Lani Morris [23]

How much do you want to directly participate in the things you call wealth? No one is completely self-sufficient – you don't garden without a shovel and if you're gardening, you're likely not mining ore and making shovel blades. Sometimes we can get a bit starry-eyed about "doing it all ourselves" – that's not possible. But how many of the things that you value do you feel a need to create or orchestrate or get your hands into?

Example: Is music something that stirs your soul, and listening to concerts something that makes you feel wealthy? Do you want to learn to make music, or would you prefer to exchange the product of your efforts (money) for the experience of listening? Tactile experience and being extremely particular about color and fit drew me to make my own clothing – but I like sewing, so even if I had a pile of money, I'd still do it.

[23] The Map of Meaningful Work (2e): A Practical Guide to Sustaining our Humanity by Marjolein Lips-Wiersma and Lani Morris, 2017

Laodicea encourages us to be specialists in whatever brings us a paycheck and then spend that paycheck on experts in other fields. We cannot be experts in everything, but the extremity of our disassociation from the things that make life a bit more joyful isn't healthy. Homemade bread is better than store-bought, and the experience of making the bread is good for the soul as well as for the biceps.

This contemplation is not merely for the creators. If you teach, do you want to do all of it in a classroom setting, or would you like to teach a seminar to a few very interested students – students that might barter for the learning? My husband is a fixer-of-things. He gets paid for that, but he also likes to fix things around the house, and he takes pleasure in the work. He likes to buy old things and restore them – that's one of the things that brings him joy – wealth – in life.

Connectors-of-people get pleasure from organizing parties and introducing friends to one another so that those friends can go on to be movers and shakers. Creating community bonds and resting in the pleasure of association makes you an influencer – one who isn't measured by clicks, but by lives changed.

Life is not meant to be lived in a one-dimensional, specialized window. Just like repetitive motion degrades our joints and wrecks our posture, repetitive lives limit us and destroy us by degrees. One of the greatest joys in leaving Laodicea behind is ripping the blinders off and seeing the world around us – all the possibilities, all the beauty, all the ways we can touch it. This world was made for us to enjoy, to indwell, to steward. We are not meant to limit our exposure to a grey cubicle and an endless succession of screens for work, entertainment, and friendship.

Following Our True Desires

"Belief manifests itself not in ideological dogma but in how we spend our time and energy. Show me what you do, and I will tell you what you believe." - Martin Schleske[24]

Whether it was 2020, when everyone's life was interrupted, or if it was something else, we've all had the moment when the world shook, and the scales fell from our eyes. We admitted that we wanted something different, we don't want to race around after a bit of cheese. We want more! We're not rats, we're human beings –created to do more than rush after transitory reward and sleep.

I don't want to live in Laodicea anymore. I don't believe that the most important things in life fill bank accounts and social media pages. But the pressure is real – that constant pressure to earn "enough", do "enough", push "enough" – with no definition of "enough". That's our problem – we don't know what enough looks like. How can we get somewhere if we don't know where it is?

---

[24] The Sound of Life's Unspeakable Beauty by Martin Schleske, 2020

The science folks have done the research – they found out that people make us happy, and stuff does not; that we can make positive change to the planet and live full lives; that we matter to one another, on incredibly powerful and profound levels; and that having purpose in life makes for happiness. Pity that marketing aimed at your emotions is more socially powerful than research aimed at your brain.

The data speaks loud and clear. We need other people to the degree that connection with others improves our physical health, absent any behavior change on our parts. Rejection reads as pain and joining just one group if you're solitary reduces your chances of death as much as does quitting smoking. We have data that says that people who live "modest" lives often end up with bigger piles of green paper than the people we think are doing "well".

We know that people are more important than stuff, our connections, our communities, are more important than our measure of fame. We don't act on that because our emotions – our fears, our envies, our hungers, they speak more loudly than our rational minds. That's humans for you – every last of one of us experiences this struggle. So how do we address this?

We start by doing the examination for ourselves.

Personal Meditations

Don't just read this chapter, do the inner work. Let this change you, let this make you feel. Convincing your brain that regenerative community is the way to go, and Laodicea is so very last century? That's the easy part. Convincing your emotions that it's time to get moving? That's another thing altogether. Start by doing the work.

1) What, when you do it, makes you feel like you did something worth doing?
2) What, if you think about it, are a few socially sanctioned desires that "everyone should want" that you just don't.
3) What does everyone seem to want that you think sounds fine, but not as exciting as it's portrayed?
4) Are you a creator, fixer, healer, etc? How would you describe yourself? There will probably be at least three adjectives that fit you. These may or may not match up to your current paid position.

Exercise: Make a visual collection of images that create desire. I use Pinterest for this, but you could save photos to a file on your computer or cut them out of a magazine. Here are the rules – because this is *not* a vision board:

1) The image must make you feel.
2) Put a note in the comments about what you feel/why you chose the image.
3) Take at least a month to build this pile of images. If you try to do this exercise in a night or a week, you will subconsciously influence your choices. Do a bit at a time.
4) This should be play. Let it be fun, relaxing.
5) After at least a month of compilation, review your images. Look for threads of commonality. (Probably multiple). Edit out the pictures that don't reflect truth.

Now. What do you want? Do some journalling. Go deep, let it hurt, let it make you hunger.

The Places We Live

The Work We Do

Rearranging Life

"Some economists have tracked individuals across a decade or so to see if changes in their personal income level are associated with concomitant changes in well-being. They aren't." - Matthew Lieberman[25]

I'm asking you to leave Laodicea, put the rat-race behind you, and you have the perfectly reasonable question, "How do I pay the bills?"

It's all very well and good to tell you that Shangri-La is just over that mountain, but if you don't have supplies to get there, it's just another dream. In other words, you still need a roof over your head, you still need food on the table, you still have to put gas in your car.

You're going to get the money you need by working a job, or starting a business, just like you normally would, if for no other reason than to keep your medical insurance.

Though Laodicea has a seriously disturbed relationship with work as one's whole identity, humans get personal satisfaction and self-respect from our work.

---

[25] Social: Why Our Brains Are Wired to Connect by Matthew Lieberman

Humans will always work. Work is a gift, a gift to ourselves, a gift to those around us.

We can't leave work behind when we leave Laodicea. We **can** leave work that we hate, jobs that bore us, employers that suck out too much of our time, and commutes that kill our communities.

We have to live somewhere, and the past couple of centuries have seen jobs move to cities and larger towns. Recently, they've started to spread out again.

As there is pressure from employees to have their money go farther (cost-of-living in urban areas is high) and value to employers to move to places with lower taxes, I believe we will see a continuation of this trend.

Modern technology has given us the ability to change something that wasn't working for humans. Now, in the transition, is the perfect time to speak in to this change. Perhaps we can find solutions that work for everyone. The internet is a great boon for many. With it we have access to the knowledge of centuries and communities of thinkers across the globe. Interconnectivity is at our fingertips, and this allows us greater physical freedom.

A gift from the 20th century is the physical infrastructure of roads, highways and trucks – you can have nearly anything from across the globe at your doorstep. It's not necessary to put your glass factory near the seashore, you can have the sand delivered by freight.

The future that we create is a future of our choice. We must choose with our eyes on not just this moment, but on the future we choose to create for ourselves and our children.

There can be a balance between working and participation in society. That's one of the best things about living right now – the internet allows us to learn and grow and network while we remain in the communities that we call home. Finding meaning in helping the people around you, in the way that you are best suited to contribute, is an effective way to achieve self-actualization. Yes – you can pay the bills and leave Laodicea behind you.

But that's the future we want to build, and the unseen truths that surround us.

The Places We Live   The Work We Do

Where are We Now?

"A growing body of evidence shows that meaningful workers are happy workers, more committed workers, and, in some tantalizing ways, better workers." (*Psychology Today*)

What does it mean to have meaningful work? Our first door-knock experience in COVID disturbed the status quo. Many of us were informed that our duties were non-essential, and that the world would keep turning if we didn't show up. What does that do to a person's psyche? Some industries, of course, were on temporary hiatus, as although the government considered them non-essential, their fellow citizens did not. Hairdressers, nail techs, and other personal care professionals took a break and came back strong. Other industries, like hospitality and travel, took a more profound and lasting drop.

Now we see a lot of folks who don't want to go back to their old jobs, and even more who were working and have decided to change lines of employment. 2021 was the year of the Great Resignation. 2023 saw the economy begin to show signs of wear, and people began losing their jobs. We aren't doing "normal" for a while... if ever. Since we're not going back – why not pick a new direction?

We still need to work, and we'd like that work to mean something. "Meaningful work" is an overused phrase, but it wouldn't be if that wasn't what we longed for.

What does meaningful work look like? I'm a creative and for me, work that really satisfies is work that produces a thing. I like to cook, ferment, bake – I love to put food up in the freezer or on a shelf. The satisfaction of seeing a thing that I made for the purpose of nurturing my beloveds? Nothing better. I make things that cannot be bought. Similarly, I write things that I hope will make the world a better place – my circle of nurturing and beauty extends to include everyone who reads my books. None of this is what I do for a paycheck, none of it is what I say when my doctor asks, "what is your job title?" But it's what makes me, me. This is the work I find meaningful, this is the work I wish to be defined by.

I try to fit in sometimes, try to make myself what I'm not. When I try to scootch my hours into maintenance instead of creativity, I collapse. I may scrub a floor because I love the gleam of hardwood in the sunshine, but ask me to sweep and dustmop it every day at a certain time? Ugh. I will spend days planning, digging, feeding, planting a garden – but don't think I'm going to go fuss over the angle of the tomato stems. Maintainers (I'm married to one, and yes – he finds my tendency to create and walk away incredibly frustrating) are a different breed.

Some of us try to be all things – try to be the creators and the maintainers and the guardians and the coordinators. I don't know if we think that's what we must do to be "enough" or if we don't understand that we're made to work in concert or if we just don't trust other folks or some combination – or something altogether different. But the more we walk into our work in life, the more we have to leave the other things behind us. "Jack of all trades, master of one". Just because I do not like to weed doesn't mean I don't have to figure out what to do about the weed situation or that I can ignore my garden until harvest. I do. I must clasp hands with those whose strengths match my weaknesses, not go everything alone.

And so when we ask, "what is meaningful work", we can't leave our definitions in Laodicea. "Meaningful" isn't a synonym for "produces fame" or "makes you wealthy". Meaning is found in doing what you were made to do, doing it well, and doing it as a part of a community. Meaning is found in being of service to others.

As a creator, I need to be connected with maintainers, I need to be connected with guardians, I need to be connected with watchers. I need to be connected with teachers, with healers. We need each other. We were designed to depend on one another rather than doing everything on our own.

It keeps us humble, to know that we cannot do it all ourselves. It frees us, to stop carrying that burden. Regenerative community, a return to normalcy, is all about learning to live in interdependent, long-term relationships once again. Where we put down roots, where we are employed, are a part of that picture. It's time to leave Laodicea behind as we walk forward into a whole new world.

Where We Live

"Living in a major metropolitan agglomeration somehow weakens civic engagement and social capital."
- Robert Putnam[26]

There have always been cities, there will always be cities. But how large those cities grow, how large they need to be, varies. It's time to look at the size of our cities and the distribution of our population.

Laodicea says that it might be nice to live in a small town, but that the sacrifices are just too great. In this paradigm, living in a small town means you are choosing to stay small. That's anathema to the Laodicean worldview. Laodicea says the same thing about small neighborhoods in big cities. They pull you down. But we're learning that connections and community build a strong foundation and are worth the costs in time that they incur. Laodicea has some concept of this, which is why networking is part of the job in most industries. It's just been commercialized.

---

[26] Bowling Alone: The Collapse and Revival of American Community by Robert D. Putnam, 2000

Laodicea likes a big city. There's a ton of opportunity to cut your community burdens and be flexible. You can pursue the maximum amount of cash, and you could become invisible at the drop of an address change.

What's great about cities? They're hubs for trade and manufacture and governance. These hubs feed into one another, producing markets for each other's wares, which expand into markets for luxury goods, the arts (particularly performing art) and specialty products, as well as being travel hubs, where large ships dock.

What are the costs of a city? People in a city require no fewer resources than people elsewhere. Humans must still have food and water, they still excrete waste and produce trash. Acres of asphalt increase heat and cannot absorb excess rainfall. People in tight confines experience more crime.

It is more difficult to live in a city and get the fresh air and sunlight that all humans need to thrive. Air pollution is de rigueur for cities, and disease spreads more quickly. With all the people in them, cities cause traffic congestion.

In a city, one is dependent on the transport of water and food in, trash out. If one of the lines breaks down, people die. I will not call cities parasitic, but they are certainly burdens on the surrounding environment, the surrounding towns. Cities have a cost – should we continue to thoughtlessly pay that cost?

We will always have cities, as I said. But perhaps we might look at what we are doing right now and address whether the cities we have are the right size for our future.

We don't manufacture at the rate we used to, and most of our manufacturing is not in interdependent pods – the steel refiner is no longer next door to the car manufacturer. We now have a very efficient road system, with truckers moving goods day and night from one area to another. So, since you can put your manufacturing plant anywhere, why pay the costs of a city?

It is unlikely that you're manufacturing durable goods on a large scale anyway. You're much more likely to be providing services, intellectual or otherwise, or making food or beverages. You can do those things anywhere. Big companies are starting to move away from urban centers, or at least moving to smaller urban areas, for just these reasons.

And what of the human cost? In a city, where one is in more danger from one's fellow humans, and where mobility is extremely high, it is more difficult to create lasting community bonds. In a city, one is constrained.

Our minds are set on the realities of the past, and 'cities' sound like a good idea. They sound advanced and futuristic. But let me paint you another picture – interconnected small towns. In a small town, you can know your neighbor and set down roots. You have enough other humans around to have the various services that modern life requires, but not so many that you become simply another face in the crowd.

And what if we modernized the small towns? Instead of being isolated, what if they worked together as teams – teams to make regional specialties like food or craft or industry. We don't need a city to be our hub anymore, we have the internet. We don't physically need to sit around a table to have a conversation, we can do it online.

We'd be smart to encourage travel between those small towns, travel to the hubs for the arts, and travel to different parts of the country and the world.

When people talk about the potential for returning to small towns and community life, Laodiceans think that we're doing something that one of my friends calls "history LARPing[27]". There were reasons that so many people left small towns during the 20th century, and those reasons haven't disappeared.

The small towns of the future have no reason to look like the small towns of the past – there is no reason to isolate and insulate, calcify and die. Instead, imagine small towns full of people who have chosen to be there because of the lifestyle improvement and who travel and trade freely, while in a constant exchange of ideas with like-minded people from across the planet. That would be a truly healthy community.

---

[27] LARP = Live Action Role Play. She meant that we're basically dressing up in costumes and pretending, not living in a cohesive society. It was a valid critique – which is why we need to address society as well as our own lives.

A community with the understanding that it is the flesh and blood humans you see who are most important to your well-being and that of your children, that of your elders. That community could be your daily reality, grounding you, giving you a place to set down roots and thrive.

Fresh air and water – ideas, people who haven't found their home yet, visitors who want to enjoy the local flavor, the ability to travel and communicate far and wide. The present has given us the opportunity to reduce the costs of living in a small town, but it hasn't given us the ability to reduce the costs of living in a big city.

We are on the cusp of change, so why not change things so that they are good for all?

Potential for Employers

There are pockets of the world where people live longer, happier, healthier lives: enclaves that tend to have abundant sunshine, green spaces, an emphasis on fitness and access to whole foods. "Where a person lives determines their level of happiness more than any other factor," Dan Buettner[28]

The benefits for employees to moving to smaller communities are well-established, but what about their employers? If we want to make it possible for the maximum number of people to leave Laodicea, we're going to need employment opportunities to spread back out.

One of the chief reasons cited for large companies sticking to large cities was that the top-tier executives didn't want to relocate. They too have community, and they don't want to lose it, nor the opportunities for their children to get the education and connections that they'll need to continue the family success story.

---

[28] Blue Zones of Happiness Website:
https://www.bluezones.com/about/history/

How can the movers and shakers get what they need while their employees also benefit? What if the top-level management took a page from centuries back, and spent part of their time in the cities, forming and maintaining their connections, and the bulk of their year in the smaller communities that house the companies themselves? The "season", as it used to be called, could be focused on the interconnectivity that is so vital to success.

In the meantime, the health benefits from living in a smaller community affect rich and poor alike, as do the benefits of being directly involved with the people whose lives you affect daily.

And the desire to be a participant in the public good only increases as one's pocketbook fills up – what better way to increase public good than by being an advocate for the workers that produce your goods or services?

Consider the tragedy of Flint, Michigan. When the company that employed most of the inhabitants left the town, their advocates left – and so did the money.[29] There was no one to put pressure on the appropriate government departments to make sure that the inhabitants had lead-free water, no tax dollars to ensure that making a switch to a source of water known to be contaminated wasn't needed to balance the books.

---

[29] Flint Water Crisis: Everything You Need to Know by Melissa Denchak; 2018 https://www.nrdc.org/stories/flint-water-crisis-everything-you-need-know

Living in a community that includes those workers will teach you what they really need, and taking a season in the city will enable you to connect with others to get it.

If the families of the executives at the General Motors plant still lived in Flint, or they had friends and relations left in town even after the plant moved away, how long do you think the water situation would have remained so dire?

Noblesse oblige is the idea that with great blessing comes great responsibility. Yes, you can live a 20th century life – you can live fast, live for yourself, take as much as possible and die like a dragon on a pile of gold. But how many of us really want to do that? That's so last millennium.

Today we think of our wider responsibilities. Do we not want to increase employee satisfaction, reduce our impact on the earth, and provide for generations to come?

If your business has a mission statement, as most do, why not consider including direct representation and participation in the well-being of your employees as part of that mission. You're not just improving the world, you'll improve your bottom line. Why? Because you get lower employee turnover, happier and healthier employees, employees that can deal with their own family needs without having to leave the area.

It's much like any other social interaction, when one party has an excess of something, and another party has a need, they can form a lasting alliance in the exchange. These alliances don't have to be limited to the highest levels of Fortune 500 companies, the ones who can afford a second home in the city. The legions of small-business owners can likewise make alliances from the comfort of their own homes.

If the small community that you live in excels in one area, and you want to ally yourself with another small community that excels in a complementary discipline – what's stopping you? You can form a partnership without leaving home. You don't need to leave your extended family or your friends, you don't need to sacrifice your health, you don't need to rip your children from their schools.

If you're an employer, as the cost of living goes through the ceiling, it might be worth it to you to relocate your business somewhere else. You can still get your raw materials. You can keep your most valuable employees doing remote work if they don't want to relocate. Yes, it's an up-front cost – but is it a cost that will soon be repaid? How can you use technology to improve how you do business?

One of the beauties of living in the internet age is that we can radically reduce the need for giant cities. There are multiple platforms online designed to connect businesspeople. Business doesn't need to live in Laodicea – and if we get the businesses out, more people will be able to follow.

The Return of the Big Frog

The average number of jobs in a lifetime is 12, according to a 2019 Bureau of Labor Statistics (BLS) survey of baby boomers. – Alison Doyle[30]

We used to mock the idea of being a big frog in a small pond, but as we search for lives of meaning and influence, that may be the best way to affect the most people. We can now pursue the fullest flower of achievement while living near our aging parents.

We have access to the knowledge of the world at large. We have access to jobs that don't require our physical presence. We have access to friends that we may see once or twice in a lifetime but who we communicate with every day. There is something to be said for developing and giving your finest skills to people you will see and interact with daily.

Smaller communities are desperate for people with big-city skills – skills like writing grant proposals to get money for needed infrastructure, skilled workers like

---

[30] How Often Do People Change Jobs During a Lifetime? – by Alison Doyle; The Balance, 2020 https://www.thebalancemoney.com/how-often-do-people-change-jobs-2060467

doctors and dentists and engineers. If you're someone who wants to do big things, but wants to do those big things for people you can see and touch? Perhaps moving back to a small town is for you.

If you're working from home, you get to pick where you live. Want to live in the mountains? On the plains? Somewhere you can see the stars? Somewhere you can afford to have your elderly parents live close by? Somewhere your kids can grow up riding their bikes without worrying about highway traffic? Take your job and go there.

You offer your skills to make Smallville healthier and draw more people like yourself back home. It might be a side-gig at first, or a volunteer position. Your contribution to your community doesn't need to be in organizing a bake sale – it might be in writing those grant proposals.

Maybe you do need to be in a big city. Could you choose to live in a tightly knit neighborhood in that city? How could you use technology to serve you?

Personal Meditations

This is perhaps the most immediately practical chapter in this book. If you're going to seek to change what you do or where you live, you're going to need to research and plan extensively:

1) What is it that you do to make money?
2) Do you have potential for doing something else? Any desire to change industries or jobs?
3) Do you have any side hustles?
4) Are you a business owner? If so, are you happy with where you're located?
5) Are there any other places where what you have to offer are needed? Do any of these places appeal to you?
6) Can you work remotely, or do you do your work in person?
7) How has technology given you more flexibility in the last few years?
8) Do you have family or a tight group of friends somewhere else? Would you want to live there? Do they want to live near you?
9) Ever given any thought to farming?

The Big Decision

The Big Decision

You've Decided for Community

"Civilization is an intricate and precarious web of human relationships, laboriously built and readily destroyed." - Will and Ariel Durant[31]

Congratulations! You've decided to leave Laodicea and participate in regenerative community. (Otherwise you'd probably have put this book down). You're ready to put in the work and make the changes. Now what? It's not like we have healthy communities on every corner.

You can join an existing community and take on the stewardship of that community, or you can start your own community from scratch. What you choose is going to depend on your personality, your neighborhood, and your opportunities. You have more decisions ahead. Once again, I ask you to engage in observation.

If you live somewhere that is rich in natural communities, and you plan to stay there, join one of them. You are blessed! Your community is not, and never will be, perfect, but your participation is only

---

[31] The Lessons of History by Will and Ariel Durant, 1968

going to make it better. Learning to deal with people in all their (and your) frailty is part of this project.

Go forth and start participating in Wednesday night services and doing beach clean-ups and helping with the holiday festival. Whatever it is that these people do, the people you want to be with – go do it. Meet people, make connections.

If you live somewhere there are a lot of almost-communities, and that's where you've decided to be, join one and make it richer. Your stewardship could take your city neighborhood from a group of companionable strangers and turn them into a team. Plant a corner garden, visit the elderly, include the children.

If you live somewhere where there are very few real communities, or if you're moving to somewhere with very few people, you might have to start from scratch. You'll be talking to your friends and connections – who wants this life? Maybe you'll be passing this book from hand to hand, seeing who resonates and who would prefer Laodicea. Not only who wants an intentional community, but who can come with you? You'll need starters, and you'll need folks to join along the way.

Some who do regenerative agriculture start in farmland that needs restoration[32], some folks start by building cisterns in the desert. The same goes for regenerating communities. What works to regenerate grassland wouldn't work in a desert. A permaculture

---

[32] Ex: Joel Salatin and his parents

food forest is not the same thing as a rotationally grazed field.

But both build soil, help soil hold onto water, and produce extremely healthy food. We want healthy grasslands and well-cared for orchards in this world – we don't get apples and pawpaws and grapes and plantain from a grazed field, and we don't get beef from a forest. That's a feature, not a bug.

Goals and resources differ. We don't need to be the same, we simply need to return to stewardship. We don't need cookie cutters within a community, and we don't need duplicates of the same type of community everywhere. Variety and complexity are imperative!

What are your values. What are your needs? You have to be excited about what you're building; you have to care about it. The goal for regenerative community is casserole exchange, not logo shirts. We don't need more places where we can say, "I joined" – we need more places where we can say, "I belong".

Explaining that difference might be a challenge if you live where there are a lot of people and little real community. In Laodicea, we've been brought up to think of "community" as any group of people. It's a marketing term. "Join my X community". So many counterfeits, so many people willing to live with the counterfeits because they don't have the same costs as the real thing. You'll have to do some education. If you've caught the bug, maybe this book can help someone else?

When people ask you about community, what will you tell them? What makes your little corner of the universe different? Stewardship and intentionality. Return to our agricultural metaphor. Agribiz produces food in abundance. But it has a lot of long-term consequences for our health and the health of the land.

Living in Laodicea has produced a lot of abundance, but it too has consequences for our mental, spiritual, and physical health. Stewardship is work, there's no getting away from it, but we need the fruit of that stewardship to be healthy.

Our first question on the road to community is, "are you a DIYer or do you want to join?"

DIY Community

"...links the decline of social capital to the exodus of financial and human capital." – Robert Putnam [33]

Community-from-scratch – that's that place you've always dreamt of, where you get all your besties to come, buy a huge acreage, and go make a new life together. It's the Benedict Option[34], where you draw likeminded associates together and buy a small town. It's living the fantasy of having all your people in one place and getting away from it all. Can this be done? Yes. There are any number of empty (and nearly empty) small towns in this country. There's also quite a bit of acreage.

This can be a lot like the original back-to-the-land movement and communes, communism and patchouli optional. It can be a religious group or an artist's retreat or what have you. Many of these "make it from scratch" communities fail, largely because they don't consider the necessity of getting fresh air in or the

---

[33] Bowling Alone: The Collapse and Revival of American Community by Robert D. Putnam, 2000

[34] The Benedict Option: A Strategy for Christians in a Post-Christian Nation by Rod Dreher, 2017

human needs of the people within them. But others thrive and have been around for centuries.

To start your own community, you're going to need somewhere to go that's big enough for everyone who's interested in joining and with enough room to grow. You'll need clear expectations. You're going to need a lot of material input to get it going, whether you're taking over a ghost town and bringing it back to life or buying 100 acres and inviting twenty families to come live with you. You – and everyone who's coming with you – is really going to have to want this, because the initial inputs are going to be challenging.

Who hasn't had this fantasy? Ah – how wonderful it would be if we could all be together! What are the costs? First – there's a big up-front financial cost. You have to buy the land (or the town) and then wherever it is will need up to date infrastructure. Prices here are coming down quickly (thanks, technology!) but it's still a cost and someone must take point.

Second – whoever has taken point in getting the land and arranging everything is going to have more responsibility and more status in the community, which is fair. But you must manage expectations on all sides. Don't assume anything – and the better you love the ones you invite, the fewer assumptions you should make.

Third – How are you going to get everyone to your place? You're going to need jobs and you're going to need opportunities in place and there are any number of things to crunch down and think about. Housing ...

houses either must be built or they must be repaired. Yes, you can have the dream, but it won't be free.

Communities constructed entirely by choice have to be driven by a strong guiding principle, and as we've seen over the past 50 years, those communities (religious or secular) can get a little weird. Why? Because we humans have the tendency to drive people to become cookie cutters – just like us. We set up an ideal for our communities and then we don't allow folks to "differ in the nonessentials". This begets a fear of exclusion, which leads to hypocrisy, which leads to hidden ugliness which can lead to a very depressing entry in a history book.

If this is your choice, it's time to hit those books. Hit the web. Talk to people. You've got to find out how communities that have lasted did it, and why the ones that disappeared in 10 years collapsed. Study the communities that work, and still work. Vanier's communities[35] where regular folks live together with those with profound disability are still up and going – how does that work?

There are religious groups who have thriving communities around the globe.[36] Study them. Study the broken groups of the 70s. Learn what works, learn what doesn't. Study the laws of the state you want to move to, find out the history in the area. All this is available, and thanks to the internet you can get it from your couch. If this is your dream – go for it. But

---

[35] www.larcheusa.org
[36] www.bruderhof.com

go in empowered and knowledgeable. Get plenty of people on this part of the project, including a devil's advocate or two.

A word to the wise: The better you like your partners in this enterprise, the more clarity is needed. If I went into business with my best friend, I'd make sure to get a lawyer to put our expectations down on paper. Why? Clear expectations of contributions and responsibilities reduce resentment. Who bought this land? Who pays the property taxes? How do we deal with money? What do we do with inheritance? How do we deal with folding your best friend's second cousin once removed in – and what happens if he's not a good fit? Write it down. Share it. Power trips and hidden assumptions are poison.

You'll want like-minded people as the core of your new community, but I strongly advise against having "like-minded" be externalities. You're better served in being like-minded in purpose and putting that purpose down on paper. If we're going to be in community together, we must be honest about our weaknesses as well as our strengths. Let the community lift all its members up. Your community will have ideals. Let the struggle with the ideals be real, help each other and encourage one another. Let us be "sinners together" as Bonhoeffer[37] called it, as we help each other grow to maturity.

The regenerative ethics of invitation and cross pollination are essential to communities started from scratch. If you're starting a community with just a few

---

[37] Life Together by Dietrich Bonhoeffer, 1939

families, you're going to need people to join your crew sooner or later. You're going to need new skills in your circle, you're going to need variety. How are you going to get people to join you? You'll have to invite them; you'll have to develop relationships of cooperation with other regenerative communities and with the regular people all around you. One of the fastest ways to tell a healthy community (religious or not) from a cult is that a community fosters outside-community relationships and exchanges of information.

When creating a community from scratch, it's incredibly tempting to "invite folks like me". But a community formed of only "folks like me" isn't going to be able to offer the full benefits of community. It's more of a circle of affiliation, and it becomes insular or falls apart very easily.

Again, let us look at regenerative agriculture: if you want to build in a healthy polyculture, include multiple generations and multiple levels of need/ability. No man is an island. We humans simply do not have time, even if we had the ability, to do everything – and we certainly do not have the time or the ability to do everything well. Relax and rest in to interdependence. Life is complicated, communities are complicated, all living things are complicated! And that's a good thing.

As Vanier says[38], it's not a celebration without the poor – or the disabled, or the elderly, nor the children. It's also not a community. Every member of a community needs to give, and every member needs to take. The

[38] Community and Growth by Jean Vanier, 1979

amount of give and take will never be equal from person to person or year to year – but we all need to be vulnerable enough to need and to be generous enough to offer. Having a variety of abilities to give and take keeps us grounded in the realities of life.

But this is real, messy, regenerative community – not Laodicean "community" packaged in plastic. In some seasons, we need more than we give. In other seasons, we give more than we take. The give and take is part of what makes community membership valuable over time. It's not realistic to say, "come join our community, healthy adult – we need lots of input" and not say, "bring your kids so we can help them grow, and bring your elders so we can care for them and benefit from your wisdom". It's also not regenerative community.

You'll also want to get your feet on the ground and see if the folks in the area you're considering putting down roots will accept your crew of newbies. I mean, it's a fine fantasy to think you'll be all alone, but you wouldn't want that even if you could have it, which you can't.

The folks who have been there for years, even if there are very few of them, can make your lives great or miserable. They know the land, they know the weather, they know quite a lot – but they don't know you. Bring their community value, that's a great way to start. Regenerative community can't develop without an attitude of curiosity and humility. What do your new neighbors need from you? What do they despise? Strive to be a blessing.

It's important to start new traditions, new celebrations, and new beauty from the get-go. This is the heart of your creation. Without celebration we don't have community. Without beauty, we can't have invitation. How can we help people's hearts buy in as well as their heads? To get people to stay, to get people to do the hard work of learning to intertwine, we have to make the experience joyful. There must be fun.

There's a lot to consider, and a lot of work to be done, but this is possible, and who doesn't want to see flowers bloom in the desert?

The Big Decision

Grow Where You're Planted

"...social capital is more important than a state's education level, rate of single parent households, and income inequality in predicting the number of murders per capita..." – Robert Putnam [39]

Maybe you don't want to – or can't – move somewhere remote. Maybe you've looked around yourself and said, "I love living here, but this community needs regeneration – stat!" How do you regenerate existing structures?

First – start talking to the people around you. There might be existing associations and micro-communities that you don't know about. Joining those groups and bringing new life might be just what the doctor ordered.

Second – if there's not an ethic of community where you live, i.e. it's not the cultural norm to sink down roots and invest in the folks around you, you're going to need to work on inviting people and starting new traditions. Laodicea has broken a lot of old

---

[39] Bowling Alone: The Collapse and Revival of American Community by Robert D. Putnam, 2000

neighborhoods, and new neighborhoods have grown up without any influence from the older, and healthier, norms of the past.

I live in a town with very high mobility and low commitment. Change your church, your grocery store, your job and your gym and you can start over without leaving your house. Anonymity is easy. How would I go about regenerating community?

First, I'd start with creating relationship. Then I'd invite folks to help me solve a problem. Then I'd start some celebrations and bring in the fun. And finally, I'd start talking about long-term buy-in. Enthusiasm is catching – but where I live, words are cheap. I need to do before I speak. Always be willing to show the "why bother" – make people want what you have to offer.

Find out what bothers the folks you live with most – that's the problem you need to solve together. Where I live, that's public safety. Where you live, it might be somewhere to gather or road maintenance or getting the kids home from school safely. This is where talking to people and doing your research will get you results.

Don't pick a project that's too big. I can't fix the homeless problem in California. I might be able to create a texting-tree to share house-camera data in case of sketchy characters or porch pirating. Bite off what you can chew (as a group) and tackle that – we have to get wins under our belts before we can tackle bigger issues or longer-term projects.

This will require a lot of stewardship on your part, but as you get those wins, hopefully you'll get others to participate and learn to love the people around them and the place where they live. Depending on how many community killers you must battle, this may be the easiest route to regenerative community.

The Big Decision

Join Existing Community

"[Moral Communities are] a place to which and in which people feel an obligation to one another and to uphold the local ways of being that govern their expectation about ordinary life and support their feelings of being at home and doing the right things." – Robert Wuthnow [40]

There are any number of neighborhoods across the country and in your own neighborhood that are on life-support. They would greatly appreciate the revitalization brought by new blood. If you join an existing community, you need to give respect to their values and promote that community's interests. Is that a commitment you can honor, or would you rather seek radical change? Don't be that guy – the one who starts hanging out with a group and makes everyone uncomfortable. Find your people and bless their socks off! Consider carefully – joining a community and setting down roots is serious business.

Returning to our metaphor of regenerative agriculture, if you're joining an existing community, you've chosen not to build a cistern in the desert. You've chosen to

---

[40] The Left Behind: Decline and Rage in Rural America by Robert Wuthnow, 2018

find a farm to rehabilitate. Great! It's time to do your research. What are the cultural values of the location you want to live in? What are their pain points? How welcoming are they to new people – especially to new people from your location (I speak as a Californian here – I know we're like locusts some places). What are their needs?

If you're joining a community, join a community that has values like yours but don't worry too much if they do the details the same way. Don't look for only a group of people who are strong or weak as you are, or a group of people who look the same as you do or have children the same age.

Look for a community that you need, that needs you. Look for the opportunity to engage in meaningful work for yourself and within that community. Always seek to benefit those around you. You don't have to make yourself something you are not to be a blessing – consider the food forest. Some plants bear fruit, some bring pollinators, others draw resources from deep in the earth to benefit their neighbors. The point is the benefit, not the method.

We won't become welcomed into the heart of a community by yelling about how awesome we are – let them find out for themselves. We enter community with humility. After all, if that community didn't have at least some of what we were looking for, we wouldn't be there. Show up. Be teachable and listen. Ask for help, and for advice. And if you're planning to be there for only a few years, just chill out and participate and don't try to change anything.

The Big Decision

Personal Meditations

Here are some questions to ask yourself, as you prepare to make this decision:

1) Do you like where you live now? Why or why not?
2) Do you have the time, energy, and friend group that you'd need to start something from scratch?
3) What do your finances look like?
4) Do you have extended family near your current home, or are they somewhere else? Would you want to live nearby?
5) How willing are you to cut loose from your current lifestyle – how able are you?
6) Do you love your neighborhood, but hate what's happened to it? Does your heart yearn to see it rebuilt?
7) What's your preferred surrounding – are you a city mouse or a country mouse? Are you where you'd rather be?
8) Look into baby communities in your faith, your vocation, your craft, etc. Do they exist? They might! Would this be somewhere you'd be

interested in living? Do you know anyone there, or anyone who knows someone? (Network away, my friend!) A visit would be an excellent idea.

9) Check out established communities too. It's very likely that new blood would be highly appreciated, if that new blood was ready to commit. Visit!

10) How long will it take you to prepare practically for this big change? What skills (soft or hard) can you acquire in the meantime to get it off the ground?

This is a huge decision, and you need to take it very, very seriously. Ripping up our roots constantly is anathema to helping baby communities to grow. Take your time, journal, travel, research until your eyes cross. And when you act, act with intention. You won't be perfect, but a start must be made.

Community Builders and Community Killers

Community Builder: Consistency

'Durban's Number' is the number of what the largest effective, coherent social group is for humans. It's about 150. – Matthew Lieberman [41]

If you want to get to know new people and be accepted as part of the group, you must show up consistently. Whether this is at the dog park when it opens, at church every Sunday night, next to the swings at midmorning with the other toddler mommies, you must show up consistently to be considered for group membership.

If you've chosen either "bloom where I'm planted" or "join a new community", consistency is going to be job one. You'll either be stewarding community consistently until it takes off and the ball starts rolling, or you'll be participating in community consistently until you are trusted and relied upon. Consistency is important because it says, "I'll be there".

---

[41] Social: Why Our Brains Are Wired to Connect by Matthew Lieberman, 2013

Life in Laodicea has left all of us with the conviction that everything is available – or should be – at our convenience. We live transitory, highly mobile lives, and we're used to thinking of most human interactions as somewhat transactional. "I pay for the kiddie gym, don't I?" But you can't pay for membership in the community of mothers who hang out at that gym, you have to be accepted into their group. Consistency is a way to knock on the door of established community and wait to be let inside.

What does consistency look like in action?

- ❖ Having moved into a new neighborhood, take up walking. Walk your dog or walk yourself – but walk. No earbuds, please – you need to learn the ways of the new place and let the new place learn your face. Stop and speak. If you've lived in the neighborhood for 20 years, pick a time and start walking your block. You already know when the maximum number of neighbors will be outside to speak to, that's a good time for your stroll.

- ❖ Join a church and show up every week – at the same service. Show up for a small group and pick one that fits with your lifestyle. (Church is community on easy-mode, and it's a great place to practice your skills).

- ❖ Show up to a group that's not too big and one in which you are eligible for membership. I **could** walk my giant dog through the play area at the park during toddler time, but I wouldn't be welcomed very quickly, if at all. You **can** go to a megachurch and only attend the latest Sunday morning sermon and then leave immediately – but if you do, it will take you years to have more than a nodding acquaintance with anyone.

❖ Choose a group that's the right size to notice you and fold you in. A group of 40 or fewer people is a good target size – smaller being better. Then just keep showing up. Everyone has time constraints, but the more time you can put into this project, the more quickly you will be accepted. You want to see the same people most of the time, and you want them to see you. Maximize your opportunities to build connections by being consistent.

❖ When you've struck up a conversation or two, invite people further into your circle. Perhaps meet for coffee or see a film that you're mutually interested in or ... really anything. To move an acquaintanceship to friendship, you move the acquaintanceship outside the place you first met.

Community Builder: Gifts

When either the donor or the recipient begins to treat a gift in terms of obligation, it ceases to be a gift, and though many in such a situation will be hurt by the revealed lack of affection, the emotional bond, along with its power, evaporates immediately. We cannot really become bound to those who give us false gifts. - Lewis Hyde [42]

Gifts are a way to offer connection with another person. This is the first extension of a rootlet to another plant. When we give and receive gifts as relative strangers, we're not saying, "I feel like you need a scented candle". No, we're saying, "Hello. Here I am, and I would like to initiate relationship".

Gifts begin a cycle of reciprocal obligation – one that is beneficial to all parties if done correctly. If not done properly, it becomes a burden. Because a gift is a step forward in the dance of relationship, gifting needs to be taken seriously and done properly or it will damage what you are trying to shape.

---

[42] The Gift: Creativity and the Artist in the Modern World by Lewis Hyde, 2007

Here's a safe guide to beginning the entrée-to-community that is gift exchange, at least in America.

- ❖ Nothing should be exchanged at the beginning of any acquaintance that is too valuable. You would think it extremely suspicious if a gentleman offered a young lady a diamond bracelet on the first date, even if that gentleman was a billionaire. This is why we start relationships with small gifts. Value is not necessarily monetary. It is understood that gifts are meant to be part of a relationship. Without relationship, a large gift creates awkwardness. This is why charity is best done anonymously or through the hands of an organization.

- ❖ Don't give people things designed to show off. If you are an amazing baker, don't make 300 perfectly decorated cupcakes as a "hello" gift to your new church. The effect is somewhat like walking in a room and screaming, "Here I am!". Make a batch of cookies instead. In other words, be a blessing but don't steal the spotlight. There will be a time and place when you're asked to make 300 perfectly decorated cupcakes, or someone's looking for a volunteer baker... that's the time to come in with the amazing. You want people to have the joy of discovering who you are.

- ❖ Gifts at the community level are best as consumables – food, flowers, lotion, coffee, etc. Garden produce is a great community gift! I've opened many a door with a bag of lemons.

Small trinkets are also excellent gifts – coffee cups, bookmarks, etc. They're meant to be slightly generic, just personalized enough to acknowledge your individuality, not so much as to make assumptions.

If you don't know the gift-etiquette in your new community, ask someone or check old etiquette books. Example: If someone brings you a plate of baked goods *on their plate,* you are meant to bake something else and return that with the plate and have a few minutes of chat. (This is a standard "welcome to the neighborhood" gift). At minimum you need to take the plate back with your thanks and complete the dance in person. Please note – the speed of your thanks and return gift are the most important things, it's better to bring that plate back empty than wait until you have time to make cookies. (I have made this error!)

This increased engagement with our lives and the lives of others will lead to an increased sense of belonging. To not accept a gift is to refuse connection. Take what you are given with gratitude, use it if possible. If not possible, regift it discreetly.

Community Builder: Working Together

The desire to roll up your sleeves and get things done locally is an important aspect of small-town identity and pride. – Robert Wuthnow [43]

Working towards common mission, whether that is an extension of work with public spaces or in taking care of the elders, children, or creating a celebration, is a wonderful way to draw a community together. Not only are you getting everyone in the same place, but they also get an opportunity to get to know one another and work alongside one another. This creates an environment where it's only natural to say, "hey, you want a beer?" or "I need to do this at my place" – an environment where the move toward community ongoing.

The purpose of service in the creation of a community relationship is to prove that you are willing to become a part of the whole. "What you ask of me, if I have it, I will share". In Laodicean times, it's become normal to

---

[43] The Left Behind: Decline and Rage in Rural America by Robert Wuthnow, 2018

be a taker, or to give money rather than time and service. Therefore, to prove that we are invested in a community, the community rightly wants to see that we will bring our time and talents to the table – not just our cash. The world in which we live in has left us all a little suspicious of new people. Service is a way to prove your trustworthiness.

Volunteer in humble positions. If you have a strong back, put out chairs. Pick up trash afterwards. If you don't, perhaps man the lemonade stand or fold clothes in the rummage sale. Don't push yourself forward, graciously offer your services to be used for the goals of the community. Let yourself be small at first.

Gentle is the hand of volunteerism. You don't need to be everything for everyone, but you can go a little bit out of your way and open the door for more utility later. You don't send a huge root out on first, you send a tendril. It is, much like gifts, better to do something small than make a huge statement. Here are some examples:

- ❖ Is there an elder in your new neighborhood? Clear the snow from their walk, mow their grass when you mow your own, offer to pick something up when you run into town.

- ❖ Set up chairs, pick up trash, sweep the walkway – do the dirty work, don't try for the work that puts you up front.

- ❖ Walk with a bucket and a trash stick.

Keep your eyes open for opportunities to do small things that get little credit – and do them.

Listen to what your new community needs. And when you have listened, act. Offer your skills with humility, offer to fill the holes you see. Use proper channels. After you have listened, you can say, "well, I know how to do so and so, would you like me to take a crack at it?" Put yourself at the disposal of those with whom you wish to identify and build up the group rather than raising yourself at their expense.

Laodicea has given all of us the experience of people showing up only to pursue their own ends – we're all a bit leery of folks who want to do all the things first. This is hard for those of us who dream of change, as we want to start yesterday, but no living system accepts radical change without damage. Become part of the system before you strive to change it, let it be an "us", not a "you". Service is one of the ways we engage and become part of the "us".

Our neighborhood just lost an older couple. One of my other neighbors interceded and has ended up the executor of the estate – but that estate is a mess! The old couple were hoarders, and their house is in serious disrepair, and was full of debris. The nearest relatives are a continent away.

Fortunately, my neighbor is a great guy – and a connector-of-people. He made a few phone calls and forged a pathway, and suddenly our neighborhood was full of men carrying chainsaws to clear a path to the back door, women carrying snacks and dealing with the trash inside the house, and folks willing (even happy) to park their cars in the driveway so that the squatters don't notice an empty house.

I hope you don't have a crisis in your neighborhood, but I'd wager that you have something that could use improvement. What might you build, to bring the folks in your area together? How might you invite the community to form around what you have built – to feel an attachment to it, eventually to feel some ownership for it?

You could build a museum or an art alley or an urban garden if you lived in the city. What might you do with an empty lot or an empty storefront? To bring folks in, you use beauty. Like a flower to a bee, your place draws folks in for their own benefit and the benefit of the host. Maybe you host dances or sing alongs or discussion groups.

If you live in the 'burbs, perhaps you put the permaculture ethic of sharing excess to work. Organize a gleaning team to pick excess fruit and distribute it if you don't have your own overflowing garden, and if you do, invite people to share in its bounty. Maybe your talent is with landscaping and flowerbeds – you could invite folks over for a tour one Saturday a month. Maybe you could get your neighborhood to do synchronized Christmas lights or a big Easter egg hunt for the kids?

What if you lived in the country, with tons of room? Might you designate some part of that land for a public garden? Host a corn maze in the autumn, or share your best sledding hill? Do you have a barn where you could host a dance?

These are decisions to be made corporately, as a community. Get people involved and excited from the get-go. Give everyone a job. When it comes time for you to be on the organizational team, give meaningful work to every volunteer, whether that's a 2-year-old who can gather flowers or an octogenarian who can keep the two-year-old from eating bees. Get the people together, face to face. It's easy to forget that everyone needs to contribute, everyone needs to be included – especially when you're thinking of the bottom line. The goal is to bind people together, not just get the job done.

Community Builder: Celebration

Television, it turns out, is bad for both individualized and collective civic engagement, but it is particularly toxic for activities that we do together. – Robert Putnam[44]

Celebrations are we see our hard work of community regeneration spark into life. The relationship threads have been exchanged, the work has been shared, the zucchini harvest has filled every freezer... we've gotten to know one another. Now, with that bit of trust built up, we can rejoice together. Celebrations differ from simple parties or other kinds of gatherings because celebrations are for everyone. Parties are for specific groups – they're for families or friends or business associates. Celebrations have open doors. This is the block party, this is the apple butter festival, this is the Christmas Tree Lighting, this is the 4th of July Parade.

Because celebrations are for rejoicing, a time for sharing one another's company after trust is established, it is critical that they be attended. So what

---

[44] Bowling Alone: The Collapse and Revival of American Community by Robert D. Putnam, 2000

if you aren't wild about apple butter? If that's your new locale's pride and joy – show up. Participation in the celebration tells your community that you enjoy them.

How do you deal with these moments if large groups of people aren't your thing? Show up early (or show up late) and make sure that you're seen by a few key people. Walk around, speak to folks, shake hands. Maybe be a big part of the clean up or set up committee? Find a small bit of the celebration to hook into and do that. But show up, even in a corner, even for an hour.

Celebrations bring communities together because they involve the community. In a perfect celebration, everyone is given some work to do, and everyone is included in the fun. That means great grandma and your disabled neighbor and the littlest kids, not just adults. Participation in the work is participation in the joy of accomplishment, and participation in the common work of putting together the celebration bonds the community together. To be excluded from the celebration is to be excluded from the community.

Great celebrations are long enough to have fun that everyone can participate in, and big enough that folks can drift through and find their niche instead of being stuck doing one particular thing. Celebrations require music, and it is far preferable to have music that is participatory rather than only professional. Hand around the tambourines, form a drum circle, lift your voices in song! Joining together in joy is the heart of celebration, and singing together produces that emotion.

Potlucks are a symbolic representation of a sharing of resources. Coming together around a common table expresses our willingness to come together for the common good. Enjoying that which is offered symbolizes the ways in which we embrace, celebrate, and enjoy the different individuals within our communities.

You can get farther in a relationship with an acquaintance by asking about the special seasoning on their potato salad than you can in months of casual chat. Food sharing has been a symbol of life sharing since there were groups of humans to share with – figure out a way, even if lime jello with canned pears isn't exactly your thing.

It is worth noting that Laodicea has been progressively more infected with elimination diets that separate the common table, as well as a peculiar increase in honest allergies. Now we've added a pandemic, with its prohibition on food sharing. This is, however it happened, a direct attack on community formation and maintenance. It is important that we push back, however we can. Unless you have an allergy, eat what's set before you. If you have an allergy, share your special food. If you can't do that, bring beverages. Participation in the common table is vital for community formation.

Community Killer: Othering

... when we see another person's emotional expression, muscles in our own faces immediately mimic the expression in subtle ways. Matthew Lieberman [45]

A consequence of trying to make everyone conform to an external standard of behavior is that we push people away. What does it look like when we replace communities-by-casserole with communities-by-ideology? Othering is the practice of turning Sarah and Charlie into "Them" or "They". It makes the "other" into an alien – someone with whom we don't have enough common ground to create relationship.

Othering feels safe after the last decade of increasingly divided existence. "I'm going to stay away from folks who aren't like me". People are scary, and we are capable of great evil. That's totally true. But scary or not, we humans need other humans. And all it takes is a history book to tell us what happens if we stick strictly to "our own kind" (whatever that means). Just let Mary be Mary and Bob be Bob. Maybe Juniper is a

---

[45] Social: Why Our Brains Are Wired to Connect by Matthew Lieberman, 2013

terrible person and should be excluded from your community – but don't tag everyone "like" Juniper. It's just that person. People – whatcha gonna do?

Humans are intrinsically tribal creatures. We're only capable of so many associations before we fritz out. It's one thing when we have tribes based on locale or occupation – things one can't get too stressed about, things that don't cross over. It's another thing to have lines that are based on opinions, faiths, or preferences. "Those people are…" Once you've made Sarah and Charlie into "Those People", you can say anything about them. They've stopped being Sarah with the freckles on her nose and Charlie who always has an extra mint in his pocket and are wandering dangerously close to being enemies. They're aliens – who knows what they might get up to!

We've gotten so afraid of people that we shoebox everyone. There's something called the "Overton Window", and this is a range of opinions allowed in public discourse. It's a fine thing to have that line, but in our fear, we keep drawing it closer and closer around us.

Fear makes us want to control. If we fear other people, we want to control them. But what if we let people be the interesting, unexpected, complex creatures that they are? What if we expand that window? No. I don't want to be in community with anyone who thinks it's acceptable to breed puppies to make fur rugs. However, there are a lot of hot-button issues today. If we tell everyone who takes a different position to go jump in the lake, we will quickly run out of people – good people, trustworthy people.

It seems like the best way to cope with the stress of life in Laodicea is to try to get everyone to be as much like us as possible. (Laodicea would love this – if we're all the same, we're incredibly easy to control). But if we do that, we lose the variety that we desperately need. If everyone in the world was just like me, there would be more food forests and pretty arrangements of rocks, but we'd all be very annoyed because who was going to maintain the looms to make the cloth so we could get on with the sewing? Let's not even discuss who'd mine the ore, smelt it and make the metal. And if everyone's head was like mine, everything would be ever so-slightly inaccurate, and no one would fix the faucet. No – we don't want everyone to be the same.

Our society is rampant with "others". Deprived of actual communities where we build bonds based on living and working with those around us, we try to build faux communities based on who's on whose debate team. That never ends well, just ask anyone who lived through the Cultural Revolution.

When our group membership is based on the purity of our belief, there is never "good enough". This is not an argument for not having devoutly held beliefs of one's own – I have them. This is a warning about what happens when we only speak with, befriend, or ally with those who agree with we in all things.

Community Killer: Long Commutes

Strikingly, increased commuting time among the residents of a community lowers average civic involvement even among non-commuters. – Robert Putnam[46]

In Laodicea, a long commute for a fat paycheck is considered a reasonable exchange. Housing prices are high everywhere, and in some places they're astronomical. Because of housing prices, it's not uncommon to find yourself living an hour or more away from your workplace. We're so used to it that we're like frogs in boiling water – have you ever thought what your commute does to your soul?

This is what my mornings look like: I seal myself into my metal box, turn on my favorite noise-cushion and steel myself for the moments to come. The first obstacle on my way to work is backing out onto my busy street. My back clenches as I stare down the street, carefully eyeing between the parked cars, timing the first car up to see how many seconds I'll have to

---

[46] Bowling Alone: The Collapse and Revival of American Community by Robert D. Putnam, 2000

look up the street for traffic. I whip my head around, see that I'm clear, and back out.

Having cleared this obstacle, the next to come is the unprotected left turn – most of the people driving with me don't use their turn signals, so I'm forced to read body language in their metal boxes. Will they be turning? Will the person behind me lose patience with my care? Are there pedestrians? So many variables, such high stakes. Finally, I'm on the mini highway that runs most of the way to work. Red lights, green lights, cars travelling too slowly for the road and cars weaving through traffic with no regard to safety. Watch out! Keep up!

My commute is quite short – only 10 to 15 minutes. My husband drives for 45 minutes to over an hour, depending on the vagaries of the other metal boxes and time of day. For not one moment of this time can we relax – there are no open roads. All is competition, danger, a race to a place we've been to before and will be all too happy to leave.

At the end of the day, it's all to be done again, in reverse. Now I'm tired, eager to be home, let my hair down, get on with my life. My to-do list jabbers in my head as I drive along, and every other box seems only to wish to slow my progress. I don't relate to those other boxes; I don't connect with them. There are no faces. These metal boxes are not humans. We only compete. How many times will I be cut off before I get home? How many trucks will I get stuck behind? The exercise makes other people into obstacles – it turns them into others.

Is it any wonder that the longer the commute, the less there is community involvement? For however long, we are in competition with the Others, and they are – because of the metal boxes – faceless. Anonymous. Not only that, but I must also continually steel myself to be "on" as I am driving. There is no respite.

Does mass transit improve the situation? No. Where mass transit exists, replace the tension of red lights with the tension of catching the right bus, subway, or train. A press of people, faces closed in the way of crowds replaces the anonymous metal boxes. Some of these strangers are dangerous in truth. Returning home is to return to warmth, to comfort, and to freedom. Now you may smile, now you may let down your hair. Now you may rest.

As we choose to regenerate our communities or create them from scratch, we need to examine the rest of our lifestyles. Working far away from home saps the energy from our connections. If connection building is our goal, perhaps we need to make the choice to move closer to our work, or to move our work closer to our homes.

Living where you work and working where you live keeps you invested in that place. The more time I spend far away from where I lay my head, the less emotionally involved I am. Perhaps it's exhaustion, perhaps it's the lack of interconnections. With a 10-minute commute, it exists as a possibility that I might see my co-workers out in town. With a 45-minute commute? Hardly. You've emotionally separated yourself into two people, one for work and one for home. There's no possibility of multiple layers of connection with a single human. Work people are not errand people are not gym people are not home people. It's all separated.

If you're ready to form or revive a community, encourage yourself and those who live there to work as close as possible to home. Working-from-home is a solution offered by recent improvements in technology and offers the shortest possible commute.

Community Killer: High Mobility

*...this is sobering news because the more individuals
endorse materialism as a positive life value, the less
happy they are with their lives. – Matthew Lieberman*[47]

In our youth, we're like the young trees you buy from a
nursery. Small root balls, easily transplanted. This is
when we should consider what lives we want to live,
what environs speak to our hearts, what primary
careers we want to pursue. This is when we are
seeking our place in this world. Every forest would like
to keep all its seedlings, but that's not possible if we're
to be healthy – we need exchange to thrive.

Forests evolve and change, the trees come and go,
species move in and out as conditions change, they're
in flux. Yet they remain a forest, a forest with a unique
identity. The natural, slow changes don't make the
forest no longer the forest – only disaster (human or
otherwise) can achieve that.

Mature trees are an entirely different beast. If you're
much of a gardener, you know that those mature trees

---

[47] Social: Why Our Brains Are Wired to Connect by Matthew Lieberman,
2013

at the nursery are bad bets for planting. Sure, they look great out of the box – but they're invariably rootbound. Instead of participating in the forest ecosystem, they are reliant on themselves (and outside input). And because they've learned to depend only on themselves, they don't put out roots readily, which leaves them prone to wind and rain for years after they've been transplanted. They only look strong.

Selfishness and intense individuality weaken us. They set us up for temporary improvements rather than long-term strength.

Modernity and the Laodicean lifestyle have told us that we should be like mature trees in pots – easily moved.

Trees in pots don't contribute to the health of the soil, they don't commune through the root networks, and as soon as the plants next to them get used to their shade, they're likely to leave. That's what we've been told is the good and right way to be. The costs to our own lives are long term, as we don't participate in generational community. The costs to those around us can be staggering – community relationships are based on long term reciprocity.

If there is no long term, then reciprocity is a gamble. People in smaller communities who have made sacrifices to live in places where family ties and relational history take paramount importance are right to be dismayed when they see people taking advantage of what they have built over the years. This is why you must prove your desire to be a member of a new community through consistency, service and humility.

This is a real concern for those joining communities that already exist. If your home is the new "hot place to live", suddenly you have tons of strangers pouring through your borders. Those folks say that they're there to find a new way of living – but are they? Do they want to become indigenous to your space? As increasing numbers move to a new locale, the housing prices will increase, and things will become more crowded. Will those increased numbers also bring a healthier economy, more opportunities for the natives, and more skilled hands to lift the community up? Or are those people planning to make the existing community over in the image of the place they left?

What's worse, if the new folk treat the small town like just another temporary destination, a place to be lived in and left behind, they only take from the community without giving back. A bit of tax revenue doesn't replace participation, love can never be replaced with money. A huge influx of new population – especially those that have no intent to put down roots – just pushes the ones who wish to love their land and one another apart.

I lived through this in the early 80s in SoCal, as there were so many new folks coming in that the natives bought bumper stickers to brag. What was the result? Old-school folks never got a chance to meet, there were too many strangers in the way. Our neighborhoods became richer in dollar signs, lonelier, and more crowded.

If you move to a new place – dig in those roots and become part of the land, the culture and the people. Commit.

Community Killer: Phoning it in

You have never talked to a mere mortal. Nations, cultures, arts, civilizations – these are mortal, and their life is to ours as the life of a gnat. - C.S. Lewis [48]

Laodicea has taught all of us to treat the people around us as if they were just bit players in our pursuit of money and fame. As we regenerate our communities, it will be tempting to fall back into old ways of doing life. It's hard work to participate in the lives of others, it's hard work to build a thriving society, and it's hard work to change. It is much easier to write a check and call your contribution complete.

So many of our volunteer organizations, places that we used to find community, have become shells for donations. Our contributions to community cannot be merely financial. We must put in the work. The very last thing our society needs is more piles of green paper and no hands to get the work done. Money is useful, and the ones who are blessed with it are encouraged to invest – but there's more to life than

---

[48] The Weight of Glory (essay) by C.S. Lewis, 1941

160

money, or why are you reading this book? Money doesn't build connection; it doesn't create ties.

This is a huge cultural shift that must happen within all of us as we commit ourselves to regenerative community. But this is a perfect place to subvert the dominant paradigm! The worldview – "throwing money at a situation will fix it" is false.

Another subversion that must happen is the modern tendency to treat all relationships as networking opportunities. Humans are smart – we've all lived with networking as the primary outlet for social connection. We are oversensitive to the possibility that the offer of relationship is purely selfish – or purely business – and we've had that up to our ears.

We can't treat people like things. We can't phone in our connection to those with whom we are building a community. Our relationships must be real. We can't "phone in" this project. Regenerative community is meant to touch hearts and fold us together. Holding yourself apart isn't part of the equation. You have to have skin in the game.

After a lifetime in Laodicea, people can tell if you are planning to phone it in. Do or do not, there is no "try". If you're ready to be a steward – be one. Invest your life, your heart, your love. And don't start until you're ready. The last thing we need is to loose a plague of people who think that changing the world will be easy, convenient, and tidy.

Community Killer: Gossip

There was a woman who gossiped. She went to a sage, after realizing that she had slandered someone, and asked how she could fix the situation. The sage told her to get a pillowcase and fill it with feathers. Once she did, he told her to go to a rooftop and shake the feathers out. Then he told her find every feather and put it back in the pillowcase. (Folk Wisdom – various sources)

A strong prohibition on gossip is necessary to regenerative community. In a garden, gossip is like powdery mildew – it spreads and it kills. Go ask someone who has lived in a small community about "why did you leave" and every one of them will mention people getting into their business who had no business being there. Gossip is so evil that every culture around the world has an injunction against it. Our baby communities must be carefully guarded against this disease.

Gossip will rip your community apart faster than anything else. I'm from a large town, so I always thought the "everyone's nose in your business" trope that my mom told me about small towns was a bit overstated. That is, I thought that until another of my friends moved back to the little town *her* mom lived in. My friend, over forty years old at the time, decided to stand out on her front porch after midnight. Someone called her mommy to tattle. This nonsense makes us feel unsafe and breaks trust. One of the first things we must rebuild in regenerative community is trust – gossip is absolutely not something we can afford.

If we want community back, if we want to draw people to small towns, small groups, if we want to form bonds, this is not the way to get there. This is an accelerator pedal on "okay then, bye". Every community has its standards, but even if late-night porch standing is against yours, gossip isn't a fixing tool, it's a breaking tool. We can't forget that in the here and now. Everyone has a choice. If the choice is between living with gossip and leaving – they'll leave.

Gossip is anathema.

How do we squash this urge?

- ❖ Use contempt. "I don't need to know that." "Ew. Are we really dissecting X's love life? Nah, I'm out". Etc.

- ❖ Particularly in the early wading-in stages, make it clear that it's just "not done" – if you must indulge, indulge in those who have volunteered (aka anyone on reality TV). We don't do that to OUR people.

❖ Develop a solid definition of what is and is not gossip, and exactly where the lines are. Yes, you can say, "please pray for Susie, she has illness in her family". No, you cannot say, "Please pray for Susie, that woman cannot keep a clean kitchen, and her family has food poisoning yet again".

Developing new habits will be difficult, and we'll have to have each other's backs as we go forward, but if we are determined to bring community back because of all its benefits, we can at least think about how to avoid the pitfalls of those who have gone before.

Gossip kills the bonds between people. Just don't.

Community Builders and Community Killers

Personal Meditations

We all live in Laodicea and were raised by her values. As important as it is to do a personal inventory of the killers and builders in your own life, I don't want you to get tangled up in guilt. Our observations are merely a starting point for improvement.

1) Which community builders appeal to you most? What feels most natural to you?
2) Which community killers are you participating in right now? Do you have a ridiculous commute, or do you change "hometowns" every five years?
3) Do you have any talents that you'd love to share with a community?
4) Go forth and do some research. As you study other communities and do your own reading, you're bound to learn more ways to build and more ways to destroy community. Write them down!

Here's a suggested reading list:

Bowling Alone: The Collapse and Revival of American Community by Robert D. Putnam
Social: Why Our Brains Are Wired to Connect by Matthew Lieberman
Culture Care: Reconnecting with Beauty for Our Common Life by Makoto Fujimura
Community and Growth by Jean Vanier
The Gift: Creativity and the Artist in the Modern World by Lewis Hyde
A Hunter Gatherer's Guide to the 20th Century by Heather Heying and Bret Weinstein

Values Point The Way

Values Point The Way

You Need a Map

Modern people began to equate progress with efficiency. Despite an ongoing valiant resistance from many quarters - including within industry - success for a large part of our culture is now judged by efficient production and mass consumption. We often value repetitive machine-like performance as critical to bottom line success. – Makoto Fujimura[49]

We've lost the importance of the immaterial. In Laodicea, money and fame are important, but kindness is an extra, a cherry on top. Community bonds are a want, not a need. We are so lonely. Hungry for belonging, hungry for meaning, hungry for beauty.

Hungry people are easily led. If we are going to change direction, we must find our sustenance where we want to go, not in Laodicea. We need to develop a new compass, and that compass is our value system.

The first step in our development of new ethics is the first step in any repentance – confession. We are not

---

[49] Culture Care: Reconnecting with Beauty for Our Common Life by Makoto Fujimura; 2017

where we want to be, we are not going in a sustainable, desirable direction. This thing we are doing with our culture, with our lives – it's damaging us.

So let us start by analyzing our lives, and the values that we live by. It's normal to live by values that won't stand up to a good examination under the light, especially when our lives are lived at a fast pace, with efficiency and busyness markers of virtue. We must examine ourselves, our habits, and our surroundings. This is anti-Laodicean.

The second step is to choose a new direction. Again, we can't simply turn back. Too much has changed. The path behind is gone. But we do have history books. We have books full of wars and dates and we have books full of ordinary lives. There were habits of virtue and vice in all eras. We can learn from them.

Scientists and explorers have studied humans carefully and recorded their data. We can learn from their work. It is a mark of intelligence to study things carefully. We have so much knowledge at our fingertips, it is incumbent on us to do our research. Ignorance can always be remedied, and no one person knows everything.

It's not easy to make a big change. It's ten thousand times harder when that big change is to your unconscious value system. I'm a creator, and I grew up around teachers, scientists and artists – people who valued creativity. You'd think it would be easy for me to prioritize creation in my life. It's not. There's a little voice in the back of my mind that always chitters about my to-do list. There's a voice that says, "you're not good enough" to use the "good fabric" or the "expensive spices" or even to put my ideas down on paper. That voice won't go away if I don't spit in its face and do what I need to do to make space for my creations. But I'm doing you no good, if you see what I make and think I don't struggle while you walk through your own struggles. We all do. It's part of life.

Consciously, I value time over money, quality over quantity, and beauty over glamour. Unconsciously, even though I'd like to have time, quality and beauty – I get twitchy sometimes. I must pull myself back from that, get my head right again.

Structure helps with that struggle. Writing things down. Talking through the "why" as well as the "what" of my values. I'm just me, standing in the world's current – and the world is not going the same direction that I am. It's like when I go swimming in the ocean and the current is moving. I keep a marker on the shore and readjust myself as necessary, so I don't finish my swim half a mile from where I started it. Having written values, goals, and aspirations is the marker we need to fight the current and change our lives' direction.

We have come to a time when we must take the records of the past and the maps from the intrepid and combine them – to move in a new direction, pursuing goods that will last, wealth that will not simply increase over our lifetimes, but over our children's lifetimes as well. This is why we need a new set of ethics. Some of the ethics are from the past, some are meant to develop our minds and hearts towards a new future, something entirely different.

What do people need? What do our communities need? What's important, in and of itself? And how do we provide those things better than Laodicea does, so that our communities and their members thrive?

Deliberate thought about how we live our own lives, and how we can live our lives in concert is how we will draw the map. Holding on to the values we've chosen in the face of pressure to be "normal" is our North Star. We will need this focus to bring us home.

Leaving Laodicea is a change centered around value systems. You might never physically leave your location – and you don't have to – but to get out of Laodicea, you do have to set yourself free of those values.

To become free, you not only have to find new values, but you also have to think about them, discuss them, and commit to them. The following section will discuss what I think we should do, and new ways of thinking that will contribute to our Safe Harbor. I expect that every one of you who takes this journey away from Laodicea will sit down and craft your own ideas.

Find me online and tell me about your ideas, won't you? I can't imagine a better conversation to have........

The mountain spruce teaches us to cast off whatever is dead. Things that are not right, internal intrigues that hide from the light, the retreat to dark places devoid of honesty, truth, righteousness, forgiveness, mercy, and reconciliation. A resonant, sounding life has learned to sacrifice what is dead and unjust. – Martin Schleske[50]

---

[50] The Sound of Life's Unspeakable Beauty by Martin Schleske, 2020

Intricacy

The mind tends to see things in a singularly simple,
divided way: there is good and bad, ugly and beautiful.
The imagination, in contrast, extends a greater
hospitality to whatever is awkward, paradoxical or
contradictory. - John O'Donahue[51]

Everything is more complicated than it looks.

The last 150 year period was an era of mechanization
and simplification. Having mechanized the process of
production, the Western World turned its attention to
the analysis of humans, the scientification of their
hearts, minds, and souls. The 20th century brought us
Freudian psychology, feedlots, and fast living. Our
knowledge increased, but wisdom was devalued. We
tried to take a mechanical mode of thinking and apply
it to living beings. We tried to apply it to animals, to
the soil, and to humanity.

Take that ever-present question, "do humans do what
they do because of nature or nurture?" It was hotly

---

[51] Beauty: The Invisible Embrace by John O'Donohue, 2005

debated throughout the 20th century, each camp taking a side. Now we find that both nature and nurture consist of myriad layers – is gut health (the flora and fauna that live within) nature? We know that it affects our mood[52]. Our moods certainly affect our actions. What helps our gut? A healthy diet, without too much sugar and processed food. Well, that's all nature. But – the first 1000 days of life is when we set our basic gut biome[53]. Since toddlers aren't making their own food choices, that comes back to nurture. Even further, your very DNA is affected by what your grandparents ate[54].

What? But wait – we also know that the words used around us can affect our neurochemicals[55]. Chemicals are nature, but our environment is nurture... are you confused yet? It's a good thing we were all given free will or none of us would get anywhere!

There's just too much here. You can't pull out a single strand and say, "this one, this one here – this is the most important thing. If I change this thing, I can change the whole". We've been looking at life like it's

[52] Psychology Today; Gut Bacteria Can Influence Your Mood, Thoughts, and Brain by Marwa Azab; 2019 https://www.psychologytoday.com/us/blog/neuroscience-in-everyday-life/201908/gut-bacteria-can-influence-your-mood-thoughts-and-brain
[53] Harvard Health Blog; Microbiome: The first 1,000 days by Allan Walker, MD, 2019 https://www.health.harvard.edu/blog/microbiome-the-first-1000-days-2019051516627
[54] LiveScience; Your Diet Affects Your Grandchildren's DNA, Scientists Say by Christopher Wanjek; 2012 https://www.livescience.com/21902-diet-epigenetics-grandchildren.html
[55] PsychCentral; Do Words Have the Power to Change Your Brain? by Cathy Lovering; 2022; https://psychcentral.com/blog/words-can-change-your-brain

a rope – three strands, maybe five, and all going the same direction. I just need to be on top of my career, my family, my health, and my spirituality to be a whole person. Done. Make a list (preferably a short one), run down the list, check things off, get on with the next thing. Laodicea likes simple things.

A reductive worldview has its origins in the desire to clarify our to-do lists. If I know that ten things need to be done to have a good life and eight are on lock, I can freely pay my attention to the last two. Life in Laodicea allows me to pretend that the state of one thread does not affect the others, and I can put off dealing with them indefinitely and still "win".

It's a lot like what we've learned about forestry in the last ten years. We learned that there is a fungal communication network between trees. Trees use mushrooms to talk. The 'net' of microbiological activity has an incredible amount to do with the health of the soil, and the health of the soil affects the health of the tree[56]. Are humans somehow less complicated than trees? Societies simpler than forests? No way.

The 21st century could be the era of the systems approach. We look at what feeds the whole, we study, but we understand that each thread is interconnected, and what affects one affects all. I hope that we leave behind the hubris of the 20th century and understand

[56] Exploring The Underground Network of Trees – The Nervous System of the Forest
by Valentina Lagomarsino; 2020
https://sitn.hms.harvard.edu/flash/2019/exploring-the-underground-network-of-trees-the-nervous-system-of-the-forest/

that there will always be more to explore, more to learn, and that simplifying systems damages them (eventually).

Our lives are more complicated than we can imagine. Consider the story of the wolves in Yellowstone. Reintroducing wolves into the park redirected rivers. The wolves ate the lazy elk, so the elk had to become less lazy. In so doing, trees returned to the rivers. Beavers returned, building dams. The rivers ended up winding as they had a century ago[57]. (An incredibly positive takeaway here is that systems are resilient – restore them and they are quick to repair damage – how quickly the skies cleared during the pandemic quarantine is a recent example).

Humans like control. We like easy. It's hard to turn away from the magical thinking of "just change this one piece and it will all fall together" and walk towards an understanding that our lives, our souls, our selves, are designed to be part of a system. Life is a dance, not a hike. We flourish as part of a whole. Our compass needs to be recalibrated – we need to walk towards systems, not single pieces.

What's the good news? Just like introducing the wolves back into nature, the journey back into wholeness is something that improve your life with the first steps. Are you well yet? No. But you're getting there – and you can give your children, and your children's children, a better life yet.

---

57 National Geographic Educational site – Video;
https://education.nationalgeographic.org/resource/wolves-yellowstone/

It's time to return to a healthy mind, a mind that sees the world as pattern, as whole. A self that is willing to find the part of the tapestry that it is meant to contribute to and gives itself wholly.

You are needed. The world does not need automatons, the world needs you. Your individual thread with my thread, the thread of thousands more – yes, this is a complicated weaving indeed. Yet, without your contribution, the whole would be weaker. Seeing the complicated dance around us is meant to fill us with wonder and awe and invite us to participate.

Significance

The desire for a feeling of importance is one of the chief distinguishing differences between mankind and the animals. - Dale Carnegie[58]

The fourth level of Maslow's hierarchy of needs is "esteem" – and this covers both respect by others and self-respect. How are we getting our esteem needs met in Laodicea? Fame and money. Both of those are easily seen from a distance, and the pursuit of both benefits Laodicea more than it does its inhabitants. It's hard to respect someone when you don't know them, and all of us crave respect. How are we going to get that necessary valuation in our new home? We remain human, and our needs will travel with us.

When you are pursuing significance in Laodicea, you flash something highly visible, whether that be a fancy watch or a tiny waistline. Or you could pretend to have lots of friends – what else is social media? Just a short cut to fame. When you don't really know anyone, because you don't have any long-term, deep relationships with anyone, you can't develop a deeper

---

58 How to Win Friends and Influence People by Dale Carnegie; 1936

respect relationship with them. We're all ripe for the picking, ripe to be sold the latest facial injection, the latest car, the latest... whatever. It's only natural.

We've borne the burden of feeling guilty about wanting these things when that's how we're made – no, not to be materialists, but to want the respect of those around us. How about we stand up and say, "stop selling us a lie!"

We know the price of fame, the cost of keeping up with the Joneses. We all know that it's not real, and that bombs our chances of developing self-respect. What are our choices? When I look out and observe the folks around me, I see two kinds of people – those who have bought into this lie and are chasing it – and those who have bought into this lie and have given up trying.

There are vanishingly few who pursue significance outside of the Laodicean norm. Those are the people I want to emulate. We need to change how we see significance and how we pursue our need to feel significant.

Let us give respect – in person, online, and in tangible ways – to those who bring meaning and happiness not only to themselves, but to those around them, and into their environments. Giving respect costs us nothing, perhaps a few seconds, but it is a powerful way to fight against the value system that Laodicea has pressed upon us. Every time we lift up a steward, an artist, a protector, a patriarch, a farmer instead of the latest celebrity, we're telling the world what we value. Because our world is now interconnected, that gives our inevitable audience a chance to peek into the lives which are truly making a difference. Significance is something that we give in concert and helps us align ourselves with our new direction.

If we cannot give respect, if we cannot acknowledge those who are significant in our lives, we cannot expect to receive it. If we leave this need unfilled, we will find ourselves running back to money and fame – even if they're false fronts, they're better than nothing. We must learn to appreciate people, including ourselves, differently to make a new way of life.

Stewardship

When we care for and love a parcel of land, we approach it very differently than if we simply consider it as a transactional commodity. Even if two neighbors don't see eye to eye on the use of their fields, if each one cares for their land, they can pursue the same larger goal - to leave the land for their children and grandchildren to enjoy. – Makoto Fujimura[59]

An extremely fulfilling way to live our lives is to put our time and energy into taking care of what – and who – surrounds us. This world requires constant maintenance to run properly, as do our relationships with others and our lives as a whole. The people who find significance in stewarding what surrounds them have wisdom and are worthy of our respect and emulation.

The first thing that those wise people have is an understanding in the difference between

---

[59] Culture Care: Reconnecting with Beauty for Our Common Life by Makoto Fujimura; 2017

stewardship and ownership. Ownership says, "this thing is my thing. I can use it up, I can destroy it, I can change it beyond recognition". When we speak of fabric, toothpaste, or hairdryers, "ownership" is the correct metaphor. When we speak of land or community, we need to use the word "stewardship".

A steward uses the fruits of the land and experiences the benefits of the community. They make changes with an eye to making the land more fruitful, healthier and more beautiful. They change their community to make it safer, more loving, more interesting. Stewards "take ownership" of their surroundings, but they consider the ones whose hands into they will leave the land, and they strive to leave that person with something better than that with which they started.

Love of Home and Love of Land, which we will address presently, pour naturally into Stewardship – for a steward loves his home, and loves the land. Someone with a steward's heart doesn't want to see what surrounds him get used up. She wants to see it grow and benefit more and more of those around her. "This good thing – let it continue to be good. Let it, in fact, grow to be better. Let my hands guide it, let my sweat push it, let my love light it with beauty".

A steward thinks not first of his own needs or wants, her first consideration is on how actions taken today will affect the owner. For those of us who are religious, we have God as our compass, and His rules as our guides in wise stewardship. For those of us who are not, we can consider future generations as the owners, and act accordingly.

Let's look at the green mantra: reduce, reuse, recycle. The neglected first part of this is "reduce". If you buy things seldom, and only buy things that you love, you're more likely to wear the items out in normal use. This is a part of stewardship – wear it out, use it up.

Those who value the environment can inhabit significance in their stewardship of the land and of its resources. Maybe such a person could organize a place in the community to share reusable resources like old cotton t-shirts or scrap wood. Then he or she could get the social reward of respect from people and the inner satisfaction of a job well done.

Those who are blessed with the ability to care for people can steward hearts. They're the ones who touch base and check in on their elders, their sick, their bereaved. This precious person is often invisible in Laodicea, and yet their value to their community is immeasurable. As we develop new ways of being, giving respect where it is due will take us far.

If we want to further the cause of regenerative community, teaching ourselves to praise others for stewardship is a good first step. We could say things like, "That person over there – look at how well he's taken care of his land!" "Look at her – she really shepherds her group of friends, they're the better for her involvement in their lives!". "Look at them, their family is really working together to take care of each other, and that care spills over to everyone around them!"

Love of Home

Just as people identify the house they live in as home, residents of small rural towns tend to identify the community as home. - Robert Wuthnow[60]

Regenerative community requires that we commit to our communities, emotionally and intentionally. To draw in the hearts and minds of those who come to live with us and participate in this work, we must offer an opportunity to love. There is something in the human soul that wants to love our homes, wants to learn to love the land we live on. Loving the land you live on, loving your home – these tie you to a place. For our purposes, this tie, this encouragement to sink in roots is a good thing.

Modernity pushes these loves to the side, they get in the way of progress, they get in the way of the search for money. How many times have you heard the job advice, "go where the money is"? Your house isn't supposed to be a home, and the change that wipes out wild spaces in your hometown is just "another bit of progress". I gave birth to the third generation of our

[60] The Left Behind: Decline and Rage in Rural America by Robert Wuthnow; 2018

family in my hometown, but I can't show them the secret places that my dad knew, or even the ones their father and I discovered. They're gone. My neighbors, by and large, just consider their homes "places to be", not "places to love". This alienation from your home soil is damaging, but that's life in Laodicea – it doesn't matter what the cost is, if you bring home the cash.

This commitment, this love of home and land, is something that can feed into the desire for significance. If we become essential to our place, we can derive meaning from that. We can also praise others for being essential, for being the cornerstones of our communities. Giving others honor is a powerful tool in regenerating community.

Knowing the value of our own consistent participation in community over decades, and if possible, over generations, is key. But it cannot be a thing of the head only – we must love. We must choose with our hearts to put down roots in the place we find ourselves and make it our home.

Indeed, loving our physical home is a part of the new ethic – it is part of what creates beauty in our neighborhoods. Beauty draws others near, allows them to ask the question, "why is this place different, why are these people different?". Beauty teaches others to hunger for good things. The beauty of home isn't about curb appeal, it's about planting an oak tree for your grandchildren.

There's a difference between a house and a home. Houses are boxes in which we live. Homes are where we cry, laugh, celebrate, bleed, argue, and rest. Home is where we keep our hearts, home is where you are always welcome. A house is just a house. Homes are more than the house, homes are the neighborhoods, the towns, the communities to which we belong. A home is where you plant the trees that you hope your grandchildren will enjoy, a home is something in which you invest more than just money – you invest heart.

Loving our homes is more than just loving our houses, it is about learning to love the little things about where we live. It's the neighbor who puts on that Christmas light show every year, and the daisies in your other neighbor's yard. It's genuinely enjoying the flavor of your town, the ups and the downs of it. For example, my hometown has always been a little bit rougher around the edges than the town just to the south. And locals are proud of that little bit of rough, even as they'd prefer the consequences to ease up a bit. We don't want to be just another tourist town; we like the character of the town we grew up in. It's the mix of a little bit of this and a little bit of that that gives each neighborhood its unique quality.

As you allow yourself to love your place, you sink into that place, you become a part of it. You commit yourself to carrying the torch, to making it better, to making it truer. The love of home lights up the ways things can be made better and brings warmth to the eccentricities that every place has.

Choose your home carefully and put down roots, because as you rip yourself out of your community, you're damaging yourself as well as those around you.

The old pattern, where the young rented and moved around, seeking their place in the world, and then they found a place, purchased a home, put down roots, this is a tradition for a reason. One needs both freedom to move and a reason to stay. Fresh air, travel and the exchange of ideas are important. It is good to invite new people into the community, and that means that some of your community will leave. That is a small sadness when they haven't yet set roots, and a larger sadness when they have. The sapling is easy to replant, the mature tree leaves a hole that cannot easily be filled – as we move towards a healthier future, we must take this into account.

Some of us will choose to move no matter our life stage, but we should do it soberly, and for reasons more than convenience. We must allow our burgeoning love of home to teach us that the consequences of tearing up those roots goes farther than the difficulty of finding a new gym, church, and favorite grocery store. Our homes are our hearts.

Love of the land starts with love of home, and extends to the physical surroundings we find ourselves in. For many of us, it's easier to start with the physical than the cultural. I love the ocean, the smell of the shore, the deep blues and greens that fluctuate with the clarity of the water and the clouds overhead. I love my bit of ocean, never to be taken for granted, never to be turned away from – for she'll give you a hard lesson in respect if you do. I love the desert, the moan of the wind over the arroyos, I love the clear nights and the endless starry sky. I love picking limes in January.

Love of nature drives us to go hiking with the sequoias, strolling in the park, and growing a pot of basil on the windowsill. Most of us want to be part of nature, which is why we're not satisfied to see it merely on our screens, we want to touch it, taste it, nurture it, be surrounded by it.

It is this love that is broken hearted when it hears about global warming, dying coral reefs or sees images of the Great Pacific Garbage Patch. There is a sensibility inborn in each of us, a desire for nature to be healthy and pure.

As we leave Laodicea, we can allow these loves to come to fruition. We can find places to be where we can make homes. We can learn to love the land around those homes and bring our love of nature to bear as we choose what to prioritize and what to leave behind.

Belonging

Friendship arises out of mere Companionship when two or more of the companions discover that they have in common some insight or interest or even taste which the others do not share and which, till that moment, each believed to be his own unique treasure (or burden). – C.S. Lewis [61]

Regenerative community offers us a wonderful field to develop friendships and romance. It allows us to find companions, without whom we can never find lovers or true friends. Laodicea is so lacking in this area that adults rarely make new friends and those looking to date end up resorting to "swiping right" and using computers to connect. How much better would life be if we could meet people in a neutral space, if our connections knew their connections, and if our relationships could develop naturally?

Can you imagine a world like that, where we weren't constantly on guard, ready to be lied to, ready to be betrayed? That alone is worth giving up the rat-race!

---

[61] The Four Loves by C. S. Lewis; 1960

We will have to re-learn to talk to one another, especially out of the gate. The way we've contracted our circles and raised our defenses, we've all gotten into the habit of checking a list of "matching" opinions before we open our hearts to friendship. Strangers are scary, but the answer isn't more restriction, it's in community. We must re-learn to talk to each other.

If your goal is to find good humans, here's a primer on conversation:

- ❖ Start with conversations about common interests. This is actually a great place in conversation to talk about the problems you hope to solve (much, much later in your acquaintance). Pretty much everyone is down to complain about potholes. You are trying to build a relationship and your subtext is, "I'm a safe person, and interesting". Don't try to build Rome in a day, just get a foundation of familiarity.

- ❖ Don't bring up whatever the most contentious issue of the day is. This is the "politics" part of "religion and politics". It doesn't matter how angry you are about whatever issue is at hand – don't start there. The last year has brought more fights to the surface than you can shake a stick at. It's too easy for us to alienate one another with a single word.

- ❖ You may certainly mention that you go to church, and if asked where, answer. Never hide who you are. But Laodicea has made all of us very suspicious – no one wants to think that you're entering a relationship to "sell" religion. I am always ready to go deep and answer any questions about my faith – there's nothing I love more. But that doesn't mean I'm going to make that the why of my acquaintance with a new person. You must love people where they are.

❖ Don't try to sell anything. If you're excited about something, talk about it. But don't even hint that your conversation partner should invest in it. We're all sick unto death of being marketed to.

❖ Don't be rude. It's a very good idea to not start about how "they" are ... whatever. You never know. The person you're talking to might be a "them"!

❖ Don't swear a blue streak. Please.

Social media, a Laodicean mainstay, serves as the perfect counterexample. Instead of being filled with commonalities, it's filled with cancellation. Instead of looking for decency in other people, we look for reasons to avoid them.

And how many "friends" do you have online who "friended" you to sell you something? Yeah, me too. It hurts every time you get an invite to buy something within a month of that "friendship", doesn't it? This happened before social media, but it's faster and more common now. No one wants to matter to anyone socially as merely a sales opportunity. We must stop this cold – it pushes people away and damages trust. We don't have enough trust in the atmosphere to begin with!

You do have to be careful around strangers, and there's no one stranger than an invisible other represented by pixels. It's not unreasonable that online interactions are filled with caution. The problem comes when we spend so much time online that this becomes our norm.

We need regenerative community to open ourselves to others in the way that we were designed to, in networks of acquaintance, where actions have consequences – both positive and negative. We need to rebuild trust, rebuild networks of acquaintances, and let that framework of trust support us as we search for friends and lovers to accompany us on life's journey.

"Our sensitivity to social rejection is so central to our well-being that our brain treats it like a painful event, whether the instance of social rejection matters or not".
– Matthew Lieberman [62]

[62] Social: Why Our Brains Are Wired to Connect by Matthew D. Lieberman; 2013

Values Point The Way

Curiosity

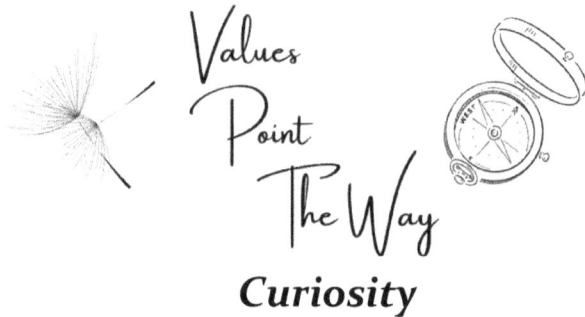

A healthy community is one that is secure, anchored in tradition and faith, but also allowing for a dynamic movement outward, sending forth artists and missionaries, caregivers and entrepreneurs. It is centered and confident in its identity as a flock because it knows the purpose for which the Good Shepherd has gathered it: to serve and bless and transform the wider world. - Makoto Fujimura [63]

How do you bring new people into your community, and ensure that your community is interacting with other communities? Encourage curiosity. If it's not just okay to learn new things and investigate new groups and try new skills, but it is expected and valued, we will see people move around within the larger community, making wider nets. We will also see people visit other communities to bring back fresh ideas and inspiration.

There has always been movement between healthy communities. Although we want to retain our mature

---

[63] Culture Care: Reconnecting with Beauty for Our Common Life by Makoto Fujimura; 2017

plantings, every gardener exchanges young plants, slips, and seeds. In regenerative community, we need the ethic of curiosity so that we go visit other gardens, learn about their specialties and exchange ideas.

Perhaps some of our young people might find that they feel the greatest belonging in another garden – fresh life is a good thing. We might, as established trees, find that some other community is doing something well, and bring those lessons home with us.

In the past, certain communities specialized in certain crafts. If you fell in love with glassblowing, there were centers where glassblowing was particularly excellent – generally because of centuries of practice and naturally good sand resources. But there are others as well – theatre, dance, song, weaving... skiing, rock-climbing, soccer... etc. The past century or so has somewhat muddled the waters, but there are still places that specialize. Why not bring this back?

Having a "special thing" and inviting others to come see it benefits the community materially, and it benefits our relationships. As we learn to appreciate intricacy and the achievements of others, we will naturally learn that it is impossible for one person – or one community – to meet all needs.

An ethic of curiosity and openness gives you not only the opportunity to explore ideas and communities as a youth, but to continue to try new things throughout your life, which gives you the opportunity to grow and change while still staying in your community. Lifetime learning is beneficial to all.

As we bring in new things, new ideas, new conversations, we keep our communities from calcification. We want to continue to pull in the best ideas from new technology, we want to take advantage of new advances in medicine, we want to learn lessons from other communities. Curiosity, openness, allows us to bring in good things. It also provides us with a center to invite others to be curious about how we're doing things.

The ethic of curiosity is designed to make learning and sharing passions, sharing crafts, a status marker. This ethic of openness extends to the World Outside, inviting them to see how good community can be. Think of how water flows in nature... the ethic of curiosity and openness keeps our pond from forming algae, and it allows us to fulfill our need to know and be known.

The ethic of curiosity isn't just to bring us good things, it's to protect us from predators. The last time that our society moved away from cities and back to the land, cults sprang up like mushrooms after a rain. Some of those cults killed people, some of them damaged them for a lifetime. We can't move forward into tighter communities without acknowledging the failures of the past. Becoming insular and walling ourselves away from the world is danger, and curiosity and movement is the preventative. Let there be light!

It's not necessary to agree with or adopt what curiosity brings you, just to listen and to learn.

Appreciation

Too many communities form, or deform, their members to make them all alike, as if this were a good quality, based on self-denial. These communities are founded on laws or rules, but it is the opposite which is important; each person must grow in their gift to build the community and make it more beautiful and more radiant, a clearer sign of the Kingdom. - Jean Vanier[64]

Our need for curiosity and variety leads right into the ethic of appreciation. How often do we really sit back and appreciate the differences between us? Laodicean thinking pushes the idea that there's an ideal for everyone, however nebulous that ideal is. If there is an ideal, then it is incumbent on all of us to be like that – not like ourselves, and not like a million different ideals.

This is, however, a big world, full of problems that need solving, full of opportunities for meaningful work everywhere. In simpler terms, if everyone bakes the

---

[64] Community and Growth by Jean Vanier, 1989

bread, who's going to build the ovens? Human trafficking is vile, children should not go to bed hungry, and we need to get the money out of politics. All of those are simultaneously true, and all of those (and so many more!) problems will take a multitude of hands to solve. There is enough mess – and enough meaning – to go around.

The problems don't have to be big ones, and the challenges don't have to be life-altering – everyday issues require everyday solutions. But great news! There are enough skills to go around, and enough different personalities. Example: Please, please – do not put me in charge of getting the people at the party to dance, chatter, mingle. Please. I'm abysmal. I'll cook. I'll plan. I'll even clean if you want... but please don't make me make with the sparkle. Someone else needs to bring their skills to bear. One person doesn't have to do everything, and they don't have to be able to do everything. That nebulous ideal? Do you think even if they could cook, clean, administrate and sparkle, that they could do all of it without collapsing? No. It's too much.

We are meant to depend on one another. We were created to work in concert, not go life alone. Why then should we be cookie-cutters, all the same? We are not worker-bees, we are not ants. We are humans! Yes, sometimes it's simply the number of hands that is brought to bear on a problem that fixes it most quickly, but that is the exception. The problems that face us societally and in our everyday lives are best tackled with a variety of skillsets and knowledge. If we are to work together, it is high time we started looking at one another and appreciating our differences.

Part of being part of a community is being able to parcel out the work – and the credit and sitting back and appreciating the talents and gifts of all the folks who were doing the work. I'll cook the food – and then I want to sit back and watch the Sparkle work the room. I get to enjoy his or her talents, s/he gets to enjoy my snacks. It's not a competition, because there is no "person who can do it all". Let us sit back and do our parts and enjoy the interplay of all our work together.

To appreciate each other is to begin to learn to love each other.

Values
Point
The Way

Leaving Spaces

It is as though beautiful things have been placed here and there throughout the world, to serve as small wake-up calls to perception, spurring lapsed awareness to its most acute level. Through its beauty, the world continually reconnects us to a rigorous standard of perceptual care: if we do not search it out, it comes and finds us. - Elaine Scarry [65]

Spaces in our lives create aeration, room in the soil around us for growth, room to send roots in all directions. The roots stabilize us, but without the space to the sides, we only grow a taproot. The tiny sideways roots hold us together, stabilize us, and make the soil itself better and healthier.

Laodicea values a life lived at super speed. Especially in the last decade, with the advent of the side hustle and internet, we're always expected to be doing something to further our goals. Prior to the plague years, I had a schedule so tightly packed that I had to make a color-coded chart so I knew where I was

---

[65] On Beauty and Being Just by Elaine Scarry; 2001

supposed to be at any given time. I was pursuing the willow-wisp of achievement. "I need to do this to get to this goal, and that to get to the other goal, and this third thing is just here because I need to eat". That's no way to live – and it took two years to get to the point where my schedule was half-way sane once again.

It's living life like a comet. Comets burn hot and they drive forward on their course with no disruption possible. There are those who must live this way – those who burn with passion that drives them to eat, sleep, and breathe their goals. Living like a comet is for the few. I wouldn't take that away from the passionate folk whose bellies burn, not in a million years. Their wings must not be clipped. But it is those few who are the heroes in our cultural story.

To fly like a star in the sky, you must cut all the weight away. There is no space in your life for tea parties, no space for card games. No space to spend a few minutes over the back fence chatting to the neighbor. And so to fly... but not all lives are lived in such a way, because not all lives can be, if life itself is to be fostered.

Again, we come to a place of retreat from the cultural norm. Deciding to make spaces in life is deciding to make room for people, conversations, random interactions. It is deciding not to fill up life with work and soma. That's what people do ... we work, we work on self-improvement, and we unplug our brains and engage in entertainment.
Leaving spaces for life is to live our values – the values of "people are important", "small things are important",

"community is important". If we don't leave space for these interactions, can we truly be said to have left the rat race behind?

I rejoice today at the outcome of a private conversation. Being home at that time was not in my plan. It was in Someone Else's daybook. I press against this constantly, being a woman of goals. If I don't see progress being made, I am brutal with myself. (How many of you can say the same? Too many, I'd guess). Today, when I would have been out, I was in. This was not my plan. But it was beautiful.

I looked up later in the morning, and thought, "I don't look up and enjoy the days as they are... I work on my workdays to get to my off days, to get to the 'days I can do what I like'. And then I don't 'do what I like' unless one is interpreting, "scrub the floor" as a hobby rather than a task to achieve a goal." Why? I don't cherish my spaces. It's not that I don't enjoy little spaces (I do) it's that I'm temperamentally oriented to diving deep into conversations, hobbies, passions – I want my big spaces to play in, and I have been convinced that I must earn that space by jamming everything else together.

But little spaces – rest breaks, time with my sketchbook, a walk with a friend – these are what inspire me to create. Time with friends gives me a reason to scrub the floor. (As an aside, I wonder how our lack of in-person socialization has contributed to messier homes that are less pleasant to live in). Why is such an important question, and if you don't leave spaces, you can never address it.

Twenty-four hours have been allotted per day since time began, and more hours were worked to put food on the table and a roof over our heads in times past. How did our ancestors make room for the little spaces? Is this a dream born of reading novels instead of history books? Is it simply that modernity inspires us to run screaming to soma for respite when war and starvation do not? Is luxury addicting more than opium?

Without spaces, we cannot get to know our neighbors, form communities, take an interest, or be known. Without spaces, we can't leave our minds free in silence long enough to create, to play, or to laugh. Spaces allow us to put down roots, roots which are desperately needed in this time of storm.

Education

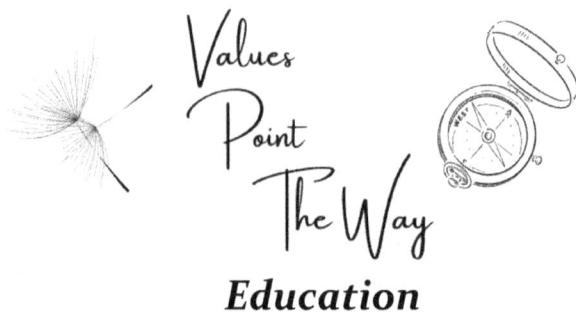

"A well-informed mind is the best security against the contagion of folly and vice. The vacant mind is ever on the watch for relief, and ready to plunge into error, to escape from the languor of idleness. Store it with ideas, teach it the pleasure of thinking; and the temptations of the world without, will be counteracted by the gratifications derived from the world within." - Ann Radcliffe [66]

Education empowers our children to live good lives. As we are in the process of redefining what a "good life" means, we will redefine education. The process of education should give significance to both the teacher and the student.

A good teacher changes the life of his students, and a student should feel as if they have received something of value after completion of the class. This is missing from most modern K-12 education, and it is one of the ways in which we are failing our children.

In Laodicea, we teach to the test. Our kids have curricula written by state officials, not their teachers.

---

[66] The Mysteries of Udolpho by Ann Radcliffe; 1794

Innovation is quashed. Values education is encouraged – as long as those values are the values of the state education authority. I watch STEM schools becoming STEAM schools and scratch my head, wondering why we've decided that English, History and Language aren't important. Civics are, after all, fairly important to life.

Higher education likewise has grown Laodicean. Where once education divided itself up between preparation for a career (doctor, lawyer, teacher, etc.) and pursuit of knowledge for its own sake (research, tenure track), college has devolved into something one simply does. Ten years ago, students could get their value in networking and internships. Now that many of our universities have embraced online courses, what becomes of that draw? Can colleges continue to charge outlandish amounts of money for classes that can be easily completed elsewhere?

Education in Laodicea rests on credentialism. In the absence of social connection and any way to know that those we hire are competent, we lean on pieces of paper to reassure us of their ability to cope. This has resulted in skyrocketing college loans, because everyone needs a certain amount of paper to acquire the "acceptable" jobs.

This situation exists because our society has grown too big. We don't know each other, we don't know who is capable and hardworking and sensible, and who is not. There's nothing wrong with credentials for doctors – but does your receptionist need a four-year degree?

The time is ripe for us to look around and consider alternative education and career paths. We know that those that work with their hands will always have work, because the physical things require maintenance. Electricity is something that no one wants to be without!

It's time to let go of the status games that value white-collar work and consider blue-collar work less than desirable. Who, after all, was considered "essential" in those months of quarantine? There were twelve pages of "essential workers" and most of those pages were filled with blue-collar jobs.

What we choose to do with our lives is going to become more holistic, not just what we think might impress the Joneses. What we do to earn our wage should fit in with the rest of our goals. Consider the plumber, who has a substantially shorter commute, which leaves him with more time and will to interact with his community. He also has entrée into every home, potentially giving him the opportunity to develop relationships with everyone in town. Let's not pigeon-hole him and tell him that he "can't be like us". No. Let's appreciate him, and if he happens to be a history buff, let's offer him classes, books, and study-groups.

Consider the beginning of public education, the ideal that every member of society could read, write, do math, and understand history so that they could be responsible members of society. This is where we need to re-build our K-12 educational system from, and there is no reason whatsoever that any of us should ever stop learning. When we have an internet full of knowledge, why should we not study everything and anything that catches our eye?

Why not have not just book clubs but restore history clubs, science clubs, and weekends learning new skills? Giving our children the love of learning, in whatever way they approach it, is valuable. Breaking out of the box could be the best thing that ever happened to all of us.

Life is not linear. Why are we preparing our children for a linear future? We know that most adults go through multiple careers and myriad employers within each. Why are we setting our kids up as if they will only do one thing with their lives? What happened to digging deeply into certain subjects and disciplining ourselves to get a solid grounding in the basics? None of us is the same, and it is time to start appreciating our differences.

Let us both value education and be willing to change the way we educate our children and ourselves.

Where We Start

True community is not produced, it is invoked and awakened. - John O'Donohue [67]

Our minds and hearts have all been damaged by living in Laodicea. The culture that surrounds us tells us that money, power and fame are the roads to happiness, and everything else is an illusion – or at least so idealistic that it's "not for normal folk". My heart has been damaged just as yours has been. My priorities constantly need readjusting. We need a compass to direct us home, and we will consult that compass often. A new ethical framework, built on the best that the past has to offer us and edited by what we have learned from doing things the wrong way and from scientific study.

Worldviews are important. How you look at the world, how you think of "good person/bad person", how you think family should be, those assumptions make up culture. There is both deep (centuries long) and shallow (a couple of decades) culture. In the West, our deep culture is based on the Enlightenment – we've

---

[67] Beauty: The Invisible Embrace by John O'Donohue; 2005

had hundreds of years of the worth of an individual, "the rights of man", etc. That's deep culture. Rooting it up, even if you wanted to do so, would take a nuclear bomb.

An example of shallow culture is what we call the "cult of the body" here in SoCal. It's been very important for the past fifty years to look great naked, and there's a lot of social status that attaches to that. In Laodicea as a whole, we believe in wealth as the primary source of value and security. We've always valued wealth in nearly every culture, but it hasn't always had primacy. That's an effect of living life without knowledge or appreciation of one another.

I sometimes see the meme that says, "in this tribe in Africa, if someone does something unacceptable, everyone sits around him and reminds him of who he really is". This appeals to our sense of mercy, and as we observe the ills of our society, we think, "sure would be nice to handle things with that kind of love". That's taking their solution out of context of their culture.

If you lived in that tribe, you'd be expected to submit to sitting in a circle while everyone you ever knew talked at you if you did something outside that tribal norm. You'd also be expected to sit in that circle and be supportive if the person in the center of the circle had hurt your sister, your wife, or your child. Because that is their norm for proper behavior.

Most Westerners would have a problem with living with that set of assumptions. I am not proposing, in beginning a new ethic, that we dig up our healthy roots – I'm proposing we pull out the weeds. Westerners enjoy individuality and individual choice. The freedom to choose our own destinies is part of who we are.

I lived in an Eastern culture for a time as a child, and I hit this head on. One day in the schoolyard I wanted to slide down the icy hillside. I didn't care that the other kids on the hillside were younger than I was – ice and snow were far from my experience, and I was enjoying myself. One of the kids my own age said, "Hey – come over here with us and slide on your feet!" I didn't want to do that. As any polite American would, I said, "Thanks but no thanks, y'all go have fun, I'll be right here!" But I wasn't allowed to keep sliding down the hill. Seven of the kids my age surrounded me, picked me up, moved me to the place of standing-and-sliding, and surrounded me so that I couldn't return to the hill. They weren't violent, they didn't hurt me, but they wouldn't relent. I was a part of their age group, and I would stay with their age group – whether I wanted to or not. I was too shocked by their outlandish action to do more than stare. This was outside my cultural expectation – kids don't force other kids to play with them in California.

Westerners are highly individualized. For good or ill, that's part of the bedrock of our culture. We have become used to a great deal of privacy and autonomy. It is necessary to participation in community that some privacy and autonomy be sacrificed – but we can't ask people to give up their individuality and get much in the way of buy-in.

Creating, sustaining and/or shaping regenerative community depends on making changes in our culture. We can't go back to the past – although we should learn from it. We can't imitate other cultures, because they don't start with the same assumptions that we do.

We should learn from them, gather wisdom, and apply it to the problems that we see in front of us, in the places we live. The desert and the rainforest do not have the same ecosystems. A small town in the deep South is going to have different challenges – and different goals – than my busy Southern California suburb.

The difference between playing at community in Laodicea and in investing in regenerative community is a new set of values. Regenerative community is about growing community in ways that will help that community – and many like it – thrive.

People dropped out of small towns and broke those community bonds for more reasons than convenience. And convenience will always be there, as will anonymity. There is always going to be a choice. Our newly regenerated communities must be so good that people just don't want to leave.

Values Point The Way

Personal Meditations

Consider this chapter only the beginning. As you prepare yourself to leave Laodicea, you will add goalposts and mile-markers to this map. Here are some questions to ask yourself, as you prepare for the journey:

1) How much Laodicea is in you, right now? No guilt! You were raised on this stuff, and you can't get away from it in your everyday life. However, some lives lend themselves to maximum rat-race, and some have a whiff of community. So – where are you now?
2) What's important to you on paper, in your ideals?
3) What would an observer say was important to you, looking at the way you spend your time and use your words?
4) Do you know how to take care of the things, people, and land around you?
5) How tightly are you scheduled?
6) Are you good at making friends/acquaintances, or is it a struggle?
7) What's your friend network look like?

8) What do you respect in other people? Both on paper and in the times you say to yourself, "I wish I was more like..."
9) Do you love your hometown, your environment, your house? Why or why not? Would you love to stay or love to go? Why? What kind of place would you go, if you could choose?
10) What values would you add to this list? Why? How do they bring you closer to regenerative community?
11) Is there anything on this list you take issue with – and why?

Your values are your compass. No one just swallows someone else's list of values whole. If you're going to get out of Laodicea, you'll need a very strong Why and a solid idea of Where To. Since Laodicea is a worldview, not necessarily a place, your map must also be of a worldview. That's where values come in – and that's why you need to do this work.

"Overwhelming pressures are being brought to bear on people who have no absolutes, but only have the impoverished values of personal peace and prosperity."-Francis Schaeffer[68]

---

[68] How Should We Then Live?: The Rise and Decline of Western Thought and Culture by Francis A. Schaeffer; 1976

Beauty

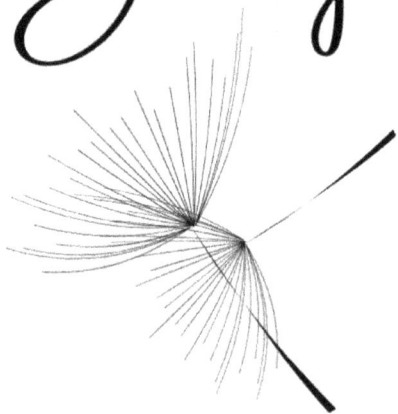

All
Around Us

Beauty All Around Us

Beauty is a Weapon

"The serious pursuit of beauty, for both children and adults, has a delightfully amplifying effect on all other areas of life." - Douglas Wilson and Douglas Jones [69]

Beauty is your secret weapon in the fight to free your mind from Laodicea. Beauty is a beacon. Beauty is an entrée into the lives of others, and engaging in the creation or maintenance of beauty gives meaning and joy. Beauty, as she is an intrinsic good, is worth making, defending, and caretaking. She is the flower of stewardship. Beauty is the hum of bees in the lavender, the fat healthy calves, the springing lambs. Beauty is our why.

Beauty interrupts our lives. In Laodicea, we've accepted that we, as peons in this system, are entitled to mounds of consumption, but not beauty. The thing about beauty is that it's more than normal. Beauty is a window into the transcendent, and as such, beauty has a spirit about it that offers something more.

---

[69] Angels in the Architecture: A Protestant Vision for Middle Earth by Douglas Wilson and Douglas M. Jones, 1998

To interact with beauty, to really see it, is to allow it to change you. To experience beauty fully, you must open your soul. This opening of the soul allows light in, fresh air. Have you ever felt fresh cold air on a wound? It stings. We avoid beauty because it stings us, it forces us to confront the parts of ourselves and our world that we'd like to ignore. Yet beauty beckons to us, calling us out. We want it, we fear it.

We hunger. The people around us hunger. Merely to pursue beauty and truth is to declare war against Laodicea. Actually to give it room to exist in your spaces, to change your life, is to step away from the culture of Laodicea. As you have made the decision in your mind to leave Laodicea but are having difficulty getting Laodicea's fingers unwrapped from your spirit, use beauty to pry yourself free. Refocus yourself on the things that take your breath away. Feed your soul and make it strong.

Beauty is a weapon to defeat the self-isolation that comes along with the pursuit of mindless entertainment. Mindless... soulless... and tempting.

Only beauty, powerful and steeped in goodness and truth, could have a chance at breaking the walls of numbing pleasure. We're all addicted to the internet. To sports. To TV shows. There is good in the discipline of taking a break from these things, but it's a hard thing to be hungry amidst a feast.

With Beauty, you're the one eating steak salad amid potato chips and soda – and it is much, much easier to make the better choice.

Bring beauty to everyday, real, physical life. That's where she is strongest. It's possible to numb oneself to beauty seen through the screen – how many pictures of the Grand Canyon have you swiped by this year? – but it takes a powerful hardening of the heart to ignore beauty in person. The call is profound, built into our bones. So then, if you will fight, fight this battle in person.

Everyone wants beauty. Lace, velvet, embroidery, exotic travel, museums, symphonies... all of this is so much cheaper now than it ever has been. Yet we live in beige. Beige is safe.

When you're pursuing beauty, if you're trying to create for yourself, you might misstep. If you're collecting objects, what you find beautiful might be annoying to your neighbor. To stop, to smell the roses makes you vulnerable. It makes you "odd". To pause in that perpetual rush towards achievement marks you out. In that moment when you allow your soul to be affected, when you allow yourself the glimpse of the transcendent, you are simply yourself – no shields, no masks. Just – you, and your real reaction to beauty. Beige requires nothing of your soul. It's easy. Beige blends in.

The concept of beauty as subversion comes straight from a fairytale... the young and beautiful maid walks up to the evil enchantress and with truth the lies come crashing down and the world walks free. Fairy tales have always been steeped in great truths, or they wouldn't have lasted for centuries. Our problem, that of exposing the comforting lie, is not new.

Beauty can be in a lovely garden, a well-made shirt, the smile of a child, the sound of a choir, the smell of sweet peas on the wind... all of these touch our lives with blessing. The moment our heroine stands up and says, "this isn't real!" is the moment the house of cards comes tumbling down. It's a time for heroes once again. Every person who shares beauty, inhabits it, creates it, is part of the fight.

To leave Laodicea is to leave the web it has spun in all of our brains. We must have a torch, and that torch – that light to guide us home – is beauty.

Subvert the Dominant Paradigm

"The enjoyment of beauty has a peculiar, mildly intoxicating quality of feeling. Beauty has no obvious use; nor is there any clear cultural necessity for it. Yet civilization could not do without it." – Sigmund Freud [70]

In 1980 when my parents and I arrived in China, the Cultural Revolution was officially over – but you couldn't tell for looking. Flowers and grass were considered decadent, pigs and geese wandering around the common areas eating off the trash piles were common. I couldn't tell you how many destroyed works of art that I saw – grass grown over a toppled statue, faces smashed off of a bas relief carved into a mountainside. Everyone wore identical blue padded jackets and pants, and almost every woman I saw had her hair cut short. Beauty was suspect.

But it was there. Under the blue cotton of those padded jackets was silk brocade in myriad colors. Under the official demeanor, my parents made friend after friend, people starving for intelligent discussions, freedom of thought. When we moved into our own

---

[70] Civilization and Its Discontents by Sigmund Freud, 1930.

219

apartment, my parents ended up throwing endless parties – officially because one had to entertain the foreigners, but my parents weren't party people. No, they'd be packed with folks desperate to have an excuse to dance, get together, laugh.

I will never forget seeing the aging couple waltzing more beautifully than many professional dancers. Both wearing their official blue padded jammies, of course. They'd learned in another time – the time when Harbin was known as the Paris of the East.

I wonder how many nights they'd danced together, quietly so as to not let on to the neighbors. How brave they were, to show so many others their skills once again.

Beauty lived on, even under the weight of the official lies. Beauty was valued, even at the high cost that might be charged at any minute, were you found out. Beauty has power.

And beauty cannot be covered in lies. Oh, I remember being taken on lots of official tours. I was greatly fortunate to be able to walk through the Forbidden City, tour the Imperial Palace up close, see those treasures which had not been destroyed – carved jade that would make a sculptor weep. I remember how annoyed the official tour guides were that we had no interest in seeing industrial factories but that we wanted to see yet more artifacts from their Imperial past. They wanted to forget those things, but we didn't.

The Cultural Revolution had tried to kill beauty, because she stood in opposition to tyranny. But beauty cannot be killed. She is in every sunrise, every sunset, every child. Beauty is power – and a ruthless government tried to stamp that power out. Yet beauty still stands, and beauty will stand when every one of those who tried to defeat her has turned to dust.

Laodicea may have infiltrated our culture, but that doesn't mean we can't do something about that. As we return beauty to her proper place, we will help others to see the network of lies in which we are enmeshed. As each person turns from those lies, the web will grow weaker. As the web grows weaker, it has less power to catch and enslave anyone.

Beauty All Around Us

Beware of Soma

"And if ever, by some unlucky chance, anything unpleasant should somehow happen, why, there's always soma to give you a holiday from the facts. And there's always soma to calm your anger, to reconcile you to your enemies, to make you patient and long-suffering." – Aldous Huxley [71]

Before we start planning our escape from the web of lies that Laodicea has woven, before we learn to wield the sword of beauty, let us examine one of the strongest weapons in Laodicea's arsenal. I'm borrowing from Huxley and calling this weapon "soma".

In **Brave New World**, soma is the government supplied drug that numbs and offers blissful escape from any unpleasantness, whether great or small. Laodicea has built up her offerings until it is nearly impossible to avoid dusting oneself with our own versions of soma. Numbing agents, stimulants, psychedelics – all of them are versions of soma. It is the purpose of mental and emotional escape that defines the drug, not its brand.

---

[71] Brave New World by Aldous Huxley, 1932

We have so many ways to dull the pain of living in Laodicea, separated from so much of what makes life worth living. Some of those analgesics are literal, as we see the opioid epidemic ravaging our country, and others are metaphorical, like our addiction to flickering screens, sugar, and other distractions. But all anesthetics make us less able to do the work at hand.

As Pink Floyd said, "we are all just comfortably numb..." As we numb ourselves, we blind ourselves to the pain of life. It's a reaction, in part, to problems from every side that we can't deal with.

North Korea is firing missiles this week. What can I do about that? Nothing. I can analyze geopolitics, but I myself have no power. Seeing problems that we can't solve is a stressor. Because of the world-wide news cycle, and because of our estrangement from our immediate communities, we are in a weird place where we see tons of problems but can't work for a solution. Not Thinking becomes a refuge. Because I see no way I can assist my fellow man, I focus on pleasure and the avoidance of pain.

Even if I am working on the problems in front of me, if I have no companion at my side, someone to take my part and have my six, I become lonely. Distrustful. Inclined to pull away from my fellow humans – for they (by their absence) have betrayed me in my hour of need. It only makes sense that I wouldn't want to interact with them, that I'd swallow beige and pull the blanket of "do not bother me" over my existence.

Ease is one of Laodicea's brands of soma. Life often makes us tired. Ease sounds so good... but ease is not rest. Rest is a period of quiet restoration after a period of work. Rest is cyclical, and it is a necessity. Ease, on the other hand, is the state where we reduce our output of effort – permanently. Choosing a life of ease is choosing a life of intoxication. Our brains grow dull, our bodies soft, our wills weak. It is with cycles of effort and rest that we become strong. Make yourself numb, make yourself small, blanket the pain your spirit is in with entertainments and luxuries... Laodicea is pleased with your self-abnegation.

Pain has a purpose. Pain shows us what must be changed. Pain points out problems. The solution to pain is not to numb it, but to deal with its cause. Sure, a shot of Novocain while the dentist drills out the cavity is good – but soma is a tin of cloves to chew while your teeth rot out of your mouth. Nothing is fixed, the waiting is just made more bearable. Flickering screens might be a fine way to spend a couple of hours, but like the sirens, the solace they have to offer comes with the danger of drowning.

We drift in a land of dreams, addicted – and who can blame us? It takes constant work not to be addicted. Soma is here, it is there, and it is everywhere. We have been sold the lie of our own smallness, our unimportance. To make ourselves forget that pain, we fill our environments with things and noises.

Any good warrior analyzes the enemy – soma is a very powerful weapon. But dangerous as it is, it is part of the cobweb. Bring enough light to bear and you can see and avoid it, bring fire and burn it, bring a sword and cut it down. Soma is sweet to taste, but it cannot satisfy. Beauty, whether sweet or bitter, satisfies the soul. As we deliver the latter, the former loses its appeal.

What Is Art?

"Art is not what you see, but what you make others see".
- Edward Degas

There's a thin line between soma – that which we use
to numb ourselves – and health. You want some
Percocet when you are recovering from surgery, but if
you have an ongoing backache, you're better off
working with the pain management team. We can't
achieve the world we need to live in if we spend our
lives distracted and/or numb.

In Laodicea, much of what is called "art" falls under the
banner of "entertainment". And most of what Laodicea
offers up as "entertainment" is soma. Designed to keep
you sitting on the couch, designed to keep you away
from your community, designed to keep you from your
life's work, the modern world consumes more soulless
entertainment than other eras could dream of. As we
wish to cut ourselves loose from the web of lies, it pays
to examine what we spend our time with – is it art, or
is it soma-tainment?

So how do we determine if something is an art form, or
soma? Art makes your soul ache. Rapturously or in

tears – art affects you, it changes you. Soma? Soma merely distracts. One doesn't want art for numbness. One does not want a sense of wonder, childlike curiosity when one is seeking a reason to rant, to vent, to choose up sides. Art may not always be pretty, but it carries the same fragrance of truth as does beauty. Art proper speaks of more than the world of flesh. Art takes you out of yourself – soma closes you in. Beauty and art open the door to vulnerable spaces in our souls.

Laodicea defends itself against art by throwing money at it. So much art is consumed by marketing, and a desire for profit and easy digestibility replaces the wild dance of beauty. Laodicea takes art – real art – and it tames it. Gelds it. Laodicea takes art and leaves the externality while removing its spirit, that which touched our hearts. It takes art and makes it into soma. Look around, there's plenty of examples surrounding us.

Pretty pictures, pleasing noises, and clean surroundings are not bad. Indeed, they are the basis for an orderly and pleasant life. But these things are simply atmosphere. The entrance to the soul comes in the moment of transcendence. And this is what we must fight for – we must fight for soul. And battle we must – this is a struggle in Laodicea. Our society is too big, there are too many eyes. In bringing things to the widest possible audience, we lose something. Yes, great art can speak to everyone – but even great art was created with a specific audience in mind.

We can create art designed for our communities and allow people to love it or leave it as they choose. We can embrace the knowledge that the person who loves a formal French garden will probably not love a tangled cottage garden – and vice versa. We don't have to choose to make either garden less like itself! As we make things "for everyone" we find that they become "for no one" – at least no one who hasn't ingested enough soma to be numb. Mediocrity is never art.

Beauty speaks past our boundaries and frees us from our pedestrian existence. It is a good thing, then, for communities to build art and beauty for all to share. It is, likewise, a good thing for individuals to open themselves with offerings of beauty. When we create art, when we create beauty, we're offering part of our own spirits to share. This offering invites community. It creates a window not only to the transcendent, but to one other.

What can you do? Make art. Make a garden. Buy art, visit gardens, look at paintings – and then let yourself be touched. Don't force it – there are no 'shoulds' in what speaks to your soul. Share your findings, share what you love, speak passionately, enjoy what you enjoy. Wake up and refuse to be numbed, seek out what inspires you and brings you to the heights. Arise, O Sleeper.

Beauty All Around Us

Stuff

"Trying to be happy by accumulating possessions is like trying to satisfy hunger by taping sandwiches all over your body." – George Carlin

Laodicea encourages the pursuit of stuff (and the status it brings). The love of money is the primary religion, after all! It doesn't matter if that purse has a pattern you don't care for, is entirely the wrong size for your proportions, and doesn't suit your sense of style – if it's the right brand, you need to own it. Beauty is far too dangerous to run around loose.

Meanwhile, we hunger for real food, made of beautiful vegetables and healthy meats, seasoned with spices and herbs with creativity and care. We hunger for food that stuns us with its color and nutrition and taste. We settle for piles of bread and soda and cookies – foods designed to addict us, designed to get us to consume more calories we need without satisfying our need for nutrition.

Laodicea lies and tells us that more stuff is a good substitute for the realness that we're craving. It uses fear as a motivator. "Will we have enough?" "Will we

ever have the opportunity to have this thing again?"
The fear drives us to grab. We cannot wait for what is
best, we grab for what is in front of our faces, simply to
have. If we don't fear lack, we fear that we won't fit in.
And status is the second face of the god of money.

And so, whether baskets or blankets or pictures or
clothes or music or smells, we acquire more and more.
We decide that we cannot have what we truly want, so
we will have as much as possible of that which we
don't. We don't buy the red dress we love, because it's
too showy. We don't wear ruffles, because they're too
childish. We are afraid to be vulnerable, to show our
hearts, to let ourselves love pretty things – and to have
them. We might become beautiful. We might be too
much. We might be too real.

Embracing beauty and welcoming it into our lives can
be the first step to leaving Laodicea. A single rose in a
crystal vase can shine so brightly that we are forced to
clean the room, and then to turn and look at the rest of
the house, and ourselves, and our souls... if we let it.

Laodicea encourages us to be careless with beauty, to
keep ourselves apart. Don't cut a single rose, full of
fragrance, from your garden and put it where you can
see it. No. Buy a dozen from a florist with no scent at
all. Put them out but walk quickly by and don't stop.
Do not engage. They're there to "be seen", not for you
to experience. More and more and ever more,
numbing us to beauty by simple force of overwhelm.

So what have we done, living in Laodicea? We've
bought. And bought. And bought some more. We

have so much extra stuff that we started using a name, "KonMari", as a verb. This refers to a Japanese organizer's method of reducing your pile of excess to have a tidier (and thus happier) life. She's not wrong. William Morris, 100 years her predecessor, was not wrong. Stuff is physical soma, numbing us, chaining us to Laodicea's value system.

So, why do we pile up stuff?
- We're trying to keep up with the Joneses. They have a new shiny, so we must too.
- We're stashing out of fear. "Enough" makes us feel safe.
- We overbought, and now we feel obligated to make some use of what we acquired. This is where you can drop into true hoarding, when you know things are trash, but you just can't let go.
- Shopping is fun. There's an itch that it scratches. It can go so far as to be an addiction. Humans have a bit of magpie in our hearts – we like new stuff just because it's new. (The shiny factor).

Stuff doesn't make you happy. Stuff can be useful. Stuff can be shiny. A particular thing can bring you joy. But piles of stuff? That's not how you get happy.

And the piles of stuff that we accumulate, the money, guilt, and time we spend accumulating them, keep us away from pursuing beauty. If I spend $40 each on 10 cheap dresses, I won't be able to afford two $200 dresses that I really love. If I spend $50/month on various streaming services, will I be able to afford to go to the theatre twice a year?

If we want to leave the webs that Laodicea has woven in our minds behind us, we must leave behind the idea that piles of anything are more valuable than what we really crave. You can pile mediocrity to the ceiling, but it will not become beautiful. Timidity, playing it safe, and acting like everyone else will not set us free.

Music and Dance

"[Music] brings you back to the mystery of who you are and it surprises you by inadvertently resonating with depths inside your heart that you had forgotten or neglected" – John O'Donohue[72]

Why is it that making music has been relegated largely to professionals? It's such a human thing, making music. It ties us together as a community, as we lift our voices in chorus. It allows us to express the deepest parts of our souls, even in private. But music, as with all other performances, has been slowly disallowed to all but the biggest frogs in the biggest ponds. No one else is good enough. And soma-tainment, mediocrity and the pursuit of the lowest-common-denominator is endless.

Laodicea is filled with cacophony, where the absence of noise is more precious than the sound of rhythm. You need never be out of earshot of a human voice. The rhythmic noise played on car stereos serves its purpose. It distracts from thoughts, it drowns out machine noise, and it provides a shield from the teaming hordes. It's not there to be listened to, to

---

[72] Beauty: The Invisible Embrace by John O'Donohue; 2005

elevate souls, to bring tears. It exists to excite, to entertain, to pacify. One need never remove one's earbuds in Laodicea. Is this the music that moves us to laugh, to cry, to dance? No. It merely entertains... soma can do no more than that.

"Noise, which alone defends us from silly qualms, despairing scruples, and impossible desires..." – C.S. Lewis, speaking as his character Screwtape[73]

Oh yes, Laodicea must have noise. Small cruelties drain us, moments of discourtesy bruise us, invisibility and mistrust lead to fear. A distraction is required. We distract with flickering lights – "comedies" that don't make us laugh, "tragedies" that don't make us cry, "reality" that is less real than a Cheshire cat.

The Bible is full of instruction to "sing a new song" and references to worship, corporate or private, incorporating song as a primary component. Music allows us to set aside our left-brain egos and exist in the moment.

But we don't sing anymore. We don't sing to entertain one another unless we're being paid. We don't sing as we work. We don't play instruments as we gather in our homes. The living-room piano is gone. The only place one finds group singing is in churches. During the pandemic, they asked churches to forgo singing – and the churches rebelled. Song is worship. It is an offering of beauty to the Creator.

---

[73] The Screwtape Letters by C.S. Lewis, 1942

Song is an offering of self. Perhaps we no longer sing because we don't want others to see into our hearts... but yet we do. We have been separated by fear for so long. Fear of one another's judgement. Fear of intrusion. But living separated leaves us weak and hungry for love. Then we put all of that love-hunger's weight on romantic love, and are inevitably dismayed when it breaks under the burden.

Just as we no longer sing, we also no longer dance. You might blame it on our Baptist forebears, but I'd take issue with that – when the churches were actively against dance, we had formalized dances, waltzes, square dance, etc. Now we dance in dark clubs if we dance at all, and that dance is primarily mating behavior. The only ones who dance outside of those clubs are professionals.

We watch professionals dance more often than we ever have. Their bodies are capable of amazing feats of skill and strength. Since we are unable to reach those heights, we restrict ourselves to observation only. We don't dance for small audiences (excepting students dancing for their parents) and we don't dance at more than a very few occasions. We limit ourselves, constricting our existence. Dance is perhaps one of the biggest expressions of "Yes" that there is! We should dance.

We need touch. Touch calms, it heals, it relaxes. Touch is reassuring and conveys emotions. The touch starved elderly have poorer outcomes when it comes to stress-related illnesses and feelings of isolation and depression. We are so afraid of one another now, so afraid not only of unwelcome touch, but that our touch may be perceived as unwelcome. This is a rich place of research – learning from the mistakes of the past but not running from the need itself. In the meantime, a gentle hand can go a long way to making the world a beautiful place. In dance, we often touch. Formalized, rule-bound, but it is touch. This touch binds us together as a community.

Perhaps we could reintroduce dance – particularly group dance, divorced from the mating game? We could introduce men's and women's event-specific dances and raise the joy levels in our celebrations. We could dance in circles or pattern dances, where partners change every few minutes. Dance is a movement of joy. This is a marvelous place to mine history and worldwide cultures for ideas. We admit our poverty and come to learn.

Are we so much richer, now that we can sit and watch someone else emote? Listen to someone else strum the guitar? I think rather that we've been robbed. We shared joy with one another, we strengthened our net of emotions, we showed one another sides of ourselves that never appear in our day-to-day lives – and we gave that away. We kneecapped our own ability to express and experience emotion when we abdicated our right to sing.

It takes will and work to get it back, and a point. You have to work to learn to use your voice well, it takes practice to play an instrument with skill, and why should you bother? You have all the biggest talents from all of history in the palm of your hand. No one wants to hear an amateur fumbling around. Yet there's an entire genre of television shows devoted to listening to amateurs do their best. How odd, it's as if the desire to connect is strong enough to fight through ennui. We want to hear what is in each other's hearts.

Perhaps listening to one another as we learn to make music is part of learning to listen to one another generally, and part of learning to appreciate the mosaic of difference in humanity. Perhaps if we returned to making music ourselves, we could regain this part of our humanity. To regenerate our communities, to regenerate our hearts, we need to bring music back to the people.

If we are to cut the ties to Laodicea, if we are to decide that we are going to embrace beauty in our everyday lives, we must learn to sing and to dance once again.

And then having learned – we must do it. Whistle while you work, hum while you drive, sing folk songs and dance a bit of a jig. It will feel dangerous, like you're committing some sort of crime. You are – against Laodicea. But to your fellow man? You'll only be opening the doors back to delight. After all, what's the worst that can happen? That they might laugh? Well then. You've given someone else a real emotion, a touchstone, you've freed them, for just one second, from the web. And the best? Well... best case, your audience might join you. Isn't that what we want? Folks to join us, as we fight free?

Music and dance are more powerful than we give them credit for. Let's take them back as our own.

Beauty All Around Us

Personal Adornment

"The media generate relentless images of mediocrity and ugliness.... Beauty is mostly forgotten and made to seem naïve and romantic." – John O'Donohue [74]

Humans need faces. Babies use mimicry and modeling to learn – they need to see our faces to develop properly. Adults use the small motions in each other's faces to interpret one another's emotions – to be empathetic. We need to smell others – that's how we pick the best mates. It's how we know if someone can become our deepest friend, or if we're always going to hold them at arms' length.

We fall in love, we weep, we cheer... faces matter. When TV showed up, we were offered limitless faces, limitless stories in the comfort of our own homes. The smiles were not aimed at us, but we felt as if they were. Screens give us facetime without the pressure of being present. But this one-way glass doesn't create community. It doesn't draw us to be our best selves. When we believe that we cannot be seen, the shadows

---

[74] Beauty: The Invisible Embrace by John O'Donohue; 2005

overtake us. We embrace invisibility – or use visibility as a crowbar to manipulate our circumstances.

You can tell how a person feels about him or herself, what venues or occasions they think are important, how that person feels about the people around them all by the way they dress. Because status and money are the gods, clothing is part of worship. Dressing well is something you do for work, for work-related events, and for the mating dance.

Commoners in Laodicea are encouraged to default to shapeless, largely colorless comfort clothes. Dressing poorly is a giant "Don't talk to me!" sign. You're communicating "I'm not pursuing wealth or fame – so I'm not going to bother". The idea that you might want to dress nicely to represent yourself truthfully or to please your neighbors' senses never occurs to us here in Laodicea.

If we adorn ourselves with a mind to reflecting our genuine personalities, rather than hiding behind a mask of sameness, we open ourselves to relationship. Our first rebellion from the webs of Laodicea is simply to connect with other people, to form relationships. It makes us so much less hungry for the offerings of Laodicean gods. Dressing well for the general public is a good first step. Not only do you serve the public, but you also reshape how you think of yourself and what you can accomplish.

But what if "they" don't like what they see? First, this is unlikely. The bar for adornment has been set at "forget me" for so long that the tiniest bit of effort is appreciated. Second, truth is important. We exist in a cloud of misdirection. Our outsides are meant to represent our insides, not paper them over. Beauty is an exercise in bringing more truth, more goodness, into the world at large.

Second, don't forget that personal adornment, like all forms of beauty, creates an opening of invitation. In our efforts to free others from Laodicea's lies so that we can get on with building regenerative communities, we will need to get as many people on board as possible. We can start by taking ourselves seriously.

How do you get someone to come to your side of the street? You can ask, you can order, you can shout... or you can invite. "We have a lemonade stand – c'mon over and give it a try!" This is one of the places where beauty comes in and does yeoman's work, beauty is made for invitations.

Invitation is a gentle art, relying on strength through vulnerability. To invite is to leave oneself open to the chance that the invitee will refuse. In regenerative agriculture, invitations are made with flowers and trees, secret places and hedgerows. We invite nature back to our farms with places to live, things to eat, bright colors and good smells. We are dependent on nature to take the invitation and make herself at home – forcing the issue (as anyone who has ever released 1000 ladybugs into their back yards only to find three the next day can tell you) is pointless. Find what is needed, what is wanted, provide that, and they will come.

What if we took that attitude to the humans around us? Opportunities instead of force. Leading by example instead of mandates. Yes, this is slower – but when we offer, when we invite, we give the invitee the choice to make themselves at home. Some will come for a moment, some will come for a lifetime – but if we have invited, it is to be hoped that all will experience joy.

What happens then, when you buck the system and dress beautifully for everyday life? You'll get stopped. Talk about an invitation to interaction! I've been stopped and asked about my clothes. Girls half my age say, "I wish I could dress like that". They're certainly not saying that I look better than they would – they're saying something else. Those around you want beauty. But if they never see it, they won't know that it's possible. Every day you have an opportunity to make a difference.

Subvert the dominant paradigm – there are no laws against wearing pretty clothes.

Architecture

"Spaces designed to incorporate light, color, natural shapes and plants have been shown to increase the health and well-being of humans using those spaces. Such spaces can increase workplace productivity and get sick patients out of the hospitals sooner in comparison to spaces without these features". – Jessi Bloom and Dave Boehnlein [75]

There is an excellent house in my neighborhood. This house sits on a corner lot between two busy-ish streets. Many a house in such a setting goes for privacy, quiet. But not this house, oh no. The house is yellow, with blue trim – and the picket fence around the house is yellow too. There were polka dots at one point. There is a "free book" mini library out front. The grass is always manicured, and what one can see of the inside of the house indicates an orderly mind.

I smile every time I pass this house. The colors, the details, the consistency – all are designed to bring a sense of whimsical joy to mind. The owner, instead of

---

[75] Practical Permaculture: for Home Landscapes, Your Community, and the Whole Earth by Jessi Bloom and Dave Boehnlein, 2015

making a try for The Most Conventional has decided to make a different statement, "Smile at My House". The statement adds to the goodness in the world.

Laodicea prefers the sameness of the housing development, all in shades of beige. It's safe – no one is allowed to have a blade of grass too long or leave an unsightly project out for public view – but it's boring. We can't have beauty in the hands of everyday people – it has to be kept as an aspiration.

I wonder – do you think that we feel we must be kept safe from the neighbors' ideas of decoration because we don't know our neighbors, or trust them? Creating beauty in the places that we live creates a sense of invitation, a visual hospitality, and predisposes our neighbors to like us. Architecture differs from building a nice garden in that architecture is the physical lines of the building itself, the materials used.

In the mid-20th century, architecture went through a period called "Brutalism", which is epitomized in the square, squat concrete buildings found in Communist countries. Like every trend, it was meant to make a statement. Although this Brutalist statement was followed by cleaner (Modernist) lines, most buildings these days are still square and unadorned. It was, again, more important to throw up lots of homes than to make the homes aesthetically pleasing.

This was not always true. Craftsman homes are both easy to live in and detailed. Other than the chance of lead paint or asbestos lingering in the corners, who wouldn't rather live in a house full of wood details?

Those houses were made to be beautiful as well as functional – and they're still beautiful. Houses from the 80s, on the other hand, are just stucco boxes with little personality. We rip them apart and reassemble them as if they were made of Legos. New houses are often not made particularly well, the walls are thin, the doors are hollow, and everything is built around a dependence on modern heating and cooling methods rather than built to suit the environment.

There are only a few of us who can afford to have a home designed to our specifications, but we all can take what we live in and make it something special.[76] Maybe we could bring back the front porch, and wouldn't that be a boon for the formation and maintenance of community?

Embrace joy in everything you surround yourself with – including your home.

---

[76] Well – those of us not in HOAs do. I'd love to see us break out of the Laodicean mindset and overturn HOA rules about beige and "appropriate" plantings and lawn décor. Wouldn't that be a move of joy across our nation? And those of us who do not live in HOAs can make our public spaces more beautiful, more appealing, more joyful.

Beauty All Around Us

Take Up the Sword

We have a sacred responsibility to encourage and illuminate all that is inherently good and so special in each other. John O'Donohue [77]

As we learn to use our eyes to see what is there, we can see the ugliness surrounding us. As we see, then we can act. We can choose. We can remake our lives. This is what the present has given us – the ability to choose. In times past, Beauty was precious, but it was costly. The raw materials were expensive. Now? The raw materials to create beauty are cheaper than they have ever been in the history of the world.

You can get your hands on silks translucent and delicate. You can work with cloth made by hand on a Scottish loom. You can obtain rare woods. You can get spices that wars have been fought for. You! You can travel more cheaply and easily than ever before in all of history. Do you go look at the world? You have beautiful faces surrounding you. Had you appreciated them before the pandemic hid them away behind masks? Life is here to be participated in. Yes, there is far more meaning to life than a good grind of pepper

---

[77] Beauty: The Invisible Embrace by John O'Donohue; 2005

on a fresh-caught salmon fillet but paying attention to that moment is paying attention to how rich you are now. And in enjoying your riches, you change.

Those who came before did not have the opportunity to choose. We do. How blessed are we! And we look away or embrace the false choice of minimalism vs. poverty. Instead of surrounding ourselves with beauty, we can surround ourselves with... nothing? As if the only choice we have is between hot-pink plastic and grey rope. This, while mahogany sits and collects dust.

We don't have the courage to break through, to become childlike, to go after what we love and not what the Joneses are decorating with. And we settle.

Settling is deadly. Beauty isn't just an optional extra. Beauty creates health. Real, measurable health. Grow a garden, sit in the sun, take care to arrange things nicely, and offer others the opportunity to spend time in your creation. It will *literally* make your life better.

Beauty is an element of hospitality. As we know that peaceful surroundings foster mental and physical well-being, our offering of a beautiful environment is a gift to our guests. As with all art, it influences the viewer to see the artist's soul, and to visit more than just their physical selves.

It is easy to keep everyone at arms' length, paint all of our houses beige, and regulate the length of the grass. That way, you can't see something that might be messy or unkempt – or something that might be unusually delightful. It's a way to keep our neighbors at arms' length – their lives, their problems, their personalities, their individuality. We can pretend that they don't matter to our lives, that we don't matter to theirs.

Invite others into spaces of beauty and see their hearts soften. Make yourself beautiful, enter Laodicean spaces, and watch their walls tremble. Beauty has become so rare that it is a threat.

We have acted in fear for so long that our reasons for doing pretty much everything come down to "if I don't then..." rather than, "because I want this in my life".

I'm not talking about ingesting modern soma, I'm talking about looking for experiences and making choices that are what we really want. I really want to go to that glass-blowing place – but I haven't. Why? I haven't let the ethic of yes, the ethic of curiosity, have their way with me.

When we live without real Yes, real Joy in our lives, we narrow ourselves and create soul hunger. That soul hunger must have its due – and it will feed at the table of soma if I don't give it solid food. We have not prioritized the deep longings of our soul. So many of us find them embarrassing. We want to sing for others, we want to write a poem, we want to walk barefoot through the forest, we want to stay up and watch the meteor shower at 2am. But we do not. We compress ourselves. Compressed, we are prey.

So, let us decompress. Let us look at those soul-hungers in the depths of ourselves and allow them some room and sunlight. Take up the sword of beauty.

Let yourself touch the bark on the giant redwood tree. Stop and smell the flowers as you walk through your neighborhood. Turn and marvel at a bird in flight. Those firmly in Laodicea's grip will look at you oddly as you choose this yes – but their reactions are their own responsibility, not yours.

Joy gives wonder permission to unfold. Wonder kills thin plastic lies. Laodicea has room for stimulants, for one-size-fits-all experiences, but it has no room for an exploration of life, of passion. If you want to leave Laodicea, you must also say YES to your hearts' desire.

Beauty is a light. It is an intrinsic good. When we make beauty, when we share it, we are taking that light and putting it out for all to see. We hold up the flaming sword and let it burn, burn away the dark that surrounds us.

Mankind has sought beauty in every form since we stepped foot out of the Garden. Even to ask, "why is beauty worth it," shows the damage our souls have taken while living in Laodicea. Beauty is our birthright. We can no more live without beauty than we can live without sunshine.

It should not require courage to embrace beauty, it should be as natural as breathing. We fight for this simply because it is right. Because we want our children's children to delight. Beauty is important.

Why beauty? Because we live.

Beauty All Around Us

Personal Meditations

Engaging in beauty is one of the most powerful things you can do to encourage yourself as you go through the hardships of leaving Laodicea, and it is one of the ways you can invite others to join you on the journey.

1) How much beauty do you engage with on a daily, weekly, monthly basis?
2) What forms of beauty speak to you most clearly? A walk in nature, the color yellow, listening to a symphony? What stops you in your tracks and induces awe?
3) What would an observer say was important to you? What beauty do you incorporate into your daily life?
4) How intensely addicted are you to soma? (We're all addicted). What forms of soma do you use, and how often?
5) Can you replace noise in your life with silence or music that you love?
6) Are you good at making friends/acquaintances, or is it a struggle?
7) How do you dress? Do you like it? What might you change?

8) What do you surround yourself with visually? Do you like it? What might you change?
9) Can you reduce the clutter and mess in your environment?
10) What forms of beauty would you add to this list? Please be creative here! I could write about beauty forever and only touch the surface.
11) Is there anything on this list you take issue with – and why?

Here's a partial reading list:

- ❖ **Beauty: The Invisible Embrace** by John O'Donohue
- ❖ **On Beauty and Being Just** by Elaine Scarry
- ❖ **The Sound of Life's Unspeakable** Beauty by Martin Schleske
- ❖ **The Creative Act** by Rick Rubin
- ❖ **Beauty: A Very Short Introduction** by Roger Scruton
- ❖ **Art + Faith** by Makoto Fujimura

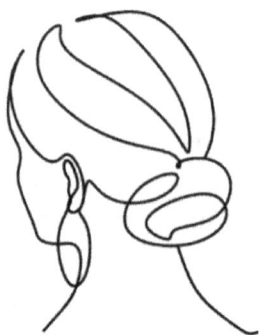

Goodbye...

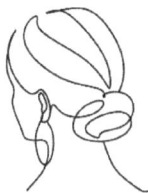

Goodbye...

Bittersweet Memories

"Our battered suitcases were piled on the sidewalk again; we had longer ways to go. But no matter, the road is life." – Jack Kerouac

The salt-sage wind blows in from the sea after the sun sets, as the distant whistle of the train blows in the distance. The mists at dawn on the beach, tide's out, and it's me and the sandpipers and endless grey - grey sea, grey sand, grey air, all the shades of grey, hit with black rocks, white birds, and the crash of waves. Camping in the desert, looking up at a sky so big it's like you're going to fall into it. Elegant desolation, hidden spots of beauty, tiny flowers between sharp points of pain - caution, caution. Redwoods so high you lose the sky, and the smell of pine. Being one step away from wilderness, even in the city, always a handspan away, touchable, gettable. Friends who always keep tennis shoes and bathing suits in their cars, ready for any adventure - because adventure awaits.

Highway 1, winding along the coast, drive slowly - you're between a cliff and the sea, next stop otters and sharks. The call of sea-lions. Every day is an endless summer, chill. Grotty restaurants that serve good food. An attitude of "let be" and independence, curiosity, peace. Backcountry full of fruit and veggies, trucks and rural reality. Snow and cactus and waves – all within a day's drive. That was the California promise.

Why do people leave their homes? There are two sets of folks on the road to la vista nueva. One set are opportunists. They're drawn to the new place because it has something they want to use – they're not looking for home, they're looking for a place to be in this moment. Another set are refugees. They're leaving something behind. They are looking for somewhere to call home. Suitcases being suitcases, they look very similar. But the refugees are the ones who tend to stay, to become part of the new place, to let it sink into their souls.

I'm a native southern Californian. I learned to ride a boogie board before I learned to read. Saltwater runs in my veins, and even a stranger can see my love for the ocean when I am in its presence. I'm a Westerner, and I love the wild. There's a part of me that smiles every time I see a coyote run down my street, even as I make sure that my cats are safe inside.

There's a part of me that cherishes the arid desolation of the high desert, that only relaxes in the shade of a pine forest. Knowing the dangers, knowing how to prepare, knowing the steps of the dance, those things make me a participant in this landscape.

Love of the land is part of who I am. It's part of everyone who grew up in a certain locale. I have memories of fishing in the lagoon with my grandpa, feeding the ducks on the other side of the same lagoon with my grandma. I walked the neighborhood streets with my mom, climbed down the sandstone cliffs to the beach where my dad taught me to bodysurf. I have place memories, ideas of what should be, based on what was.

Change comes everywhere, always. That's part of life. But the changes to my homeland have made it so that I can't share most of these things with my kids. The beach is still there, and the sandpipers still search for sand crabs. But the man-made harbor has washed away most of the sand, so where my grandfather took a walk every day, I can only walk when the tide is at its lowest ebb. The best swimming spots are crowded, crowded enough that a Wednesday morning at 10am is as packed as it was Saturday at noon when I was a girl. It takes twice as long to get anywhere – whether that's the beach, a museum, an amusement park, or out of the area. I'm penned at home by the press of people.

The promise of freedom that California dreams were built on is washing away. No more room for the surfers who worked odd jobs so they could catch the 4am break. No more crazy artists living in odd corners and making the neighborhoods unique and beautiful.

No more room for ordinary folks to live their lives – rapidly increasing housing prices might be good for my net worth, but I don't like living in a world where buying a home has become a blood sport. My next-door neighbors wept when their offer was accepted... wept for the opportunity to spend half a million dollars on a home two hours from their families and their workplaces. That's not right. And what about my kids? How are they going to make their way?

California has broken her promise – and that's before we talk about the myriad other problems that none of us from the Golden State can get away from. I'm not the only one who feels this way, and many of us are leaving.

Unfortunately, we have a reputation to live down. Seems like too many Californians bring the worst of our state along when we leave. Folks wouldn't mind if we showed up with good tans and a mean recipe for carne asada. They do mind when we show up driving like we're still on the 5, crowd their kids out of jobs and homes, and act like a plague of locusts.

Refugees need to be sensitive to the places they move to. The opportunists who come along for the ride confuse the natives, and we must bear the burden of showing our true colors. I lived through the eighties in California – I know how annoying new people can be! It is for us to be vulnerable, teachable, pliant.

If we are leaving our home because it is no longer what it once was, if we are leaving with our hearts breaking, it would be deeply wrong to give that pain to someone else who we hope to live with. Yes, our mere presence creates change, that is unavoidable. But we can choose to make the change a blessing rather than a curse.

When I get to where I'm going, after I get the boxes unpacked and the CA plates off my car, I need to get myself into my community and start learning.

It will be time for me to put skin in the game, right from the start. I will have to open my heart and learn to love again. How odious can a person be who comes alongside and asks to be shown how to love your land? The vulnerability, the openness to new experience, the tenderness – those are hard to resist. Those make it easier for the natives to open their arms and welcome you to your new home. When we leave our beloved home behind, when we say goodbye, it must be goodbye.

I will always love my home, the smell of salt-sage-wind at night. A tear comes to my eye, but goodbye is sometimes a very good thing.

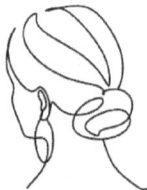 

Goodbye...

Wrapping Up

"You gain strength, courage, and confidence by every experience in which you really stop to look fear in the face. You must do the thing which you think you cannot do." - Eleanor Roosevelt

There has been a tremendous amount of research done about the human condition, about community, about how we interact socially, about what truly makes us happy and what does not. As those who developed regenerative agriculture observed nature and imitated her in a controlled fashion, why do we not take the observations we have available to us and make a plan of action, a plan to change the world?

It hurts, that moment when you realize you've been living in a network of lies. You've lived your whole life in Laodicea, and you never knew that there was another world waiting for you, the one you'd been designed to live in. In the world you were meant for, your life has meaning and purpose. Every day is filled with opportunities to interact with others and the world around you, bring light into people's lives and leave a positive mark on the world.

But you're still standing in Laodicea. A world where nothing matters, and the only goal is transitory pleasure. You know that it's a fool's game, yet you've been playing it all your life – it's likely all that you know. All your friends live here, and you've built a life on the paradigms that you were given. If you step away, things are going to break.

Most of us stand on the precipice and look for a long time before we dare to jump. We know that we won't be satisfied with lies once we taste the truth. Truth. You can look at it and walk away, or you can look at it and let it change everything in you so that you become part of it.

Moving into truth costs. Moving costs you your self-image. You had always thought of yourself as just one of the many. Now you learn that you were called out individually. You thought that how you lived your life mattered only to a select few, and now you see the ripple effect that even your least actions have on the world around you. As you see these truths, you start to feel the weight of responsibility. If what you do matters, it matters what you do.

Leaving Laodicea will cost you friendships. While you'll learn that individuals have far greater worth than you'd ever dreamt, you'll also learn to abhor that which damages those individuals. Gossip will become anathema. Toleration of sin or decay in the lives around you will drive you mad. And for you, as you pull the beam from your own eye? You might change so much that your friends won't want you around anymore. If they stay caught, they won't understand your choices, they won't understand your priorities, and they will grumble as those priorities change your path. Some might even try to grab onto you and force you to stay. Call them to follow, but don't stop.

Every moment of your old life you've been trained to want certain things. There's some strange, twisted part of us that is more pleased to want and not possess than to enjoy and not want.

Giving up pretending to want what you don't want is harder than giving up getting what you weren't going to get anyway. Taking the Ferrari off your vision board is harder than having it there and knowing that you'll never get it. In Laodicea, our wants define us. Leaving those wants behind is leaving part of oneself behind.

The fact that you're leaving wants behind to pursue true desire, leaving distractions behind to pursue purpose, is immaterial. You are still walking away, and the first steps are hard. How then, can you change? You must taste true desire. You must learn to let yourself hope for what you've always wanted.

It is time for America to rediscover her pioneer spirit. We are a nation descended from people who left everything they knew to embrace a better future. We have been imprisoned by the idea that meaningful lives aren't possible for us, but as we see the truth, we must allow that truth to free us.

We are in a time of change. Life has been predictable for decades. Even our fashions haven't changed much, just cycled around in a circle. It's not odd that, having been taught one way to be, we only see one set of possibilities. Human eyes are forever looking backward – it's like that quote about defense, "We're always prepared to fight the last war".

We've been taught to fight that last war by networking, but we weren't taught to make adult friends, and we don't know anything about how to be part of a real, skin-in-the-game, consistent community. We've been taught to pursue dreams, but not taught to dream outside the box. We've been taught to make ourselves small, safe, and quiet – not to take risks and change the world. We're short-sighted because we believe that tomorrow will just be a continuation of today.

We believed that, anyway... and then 2020 broke out on the scene. History is replete with these moments. Knocks on the door. Consider the era of La Belle Epoque. The intelligentsia thought that we'd evolved past war, that it was all going to be about making things perfect and tidy. Then World War I hit, savaging the Western world, changing it forever.

So many of us now, in this moment, are desperate to return to normalcy. But normal isn't "normal" anymore. This presents all of us with a terrific opportunity to change the things in our lives that want changing, change the things in our culture that want changing. The mooring has broken loose, and it's a time of danger – but if you didn't like where the ship was docked, now is the time to redirect her. Now is the time to pioneer.

I envision a world where cities shrink to more manageable proportions. There are a few among us who require physical closeness to a bustling metropolis, and those will stay. The wealthy can come for a season to meet and marry, and the rest? Well, we'll be where we can make the connections that benefit us.

I envision a future where bedroom communities remake themselves into stand-alone towns, and likewise start to shrink as fewer people are choosing a long commute into a city. As work-from-home becomes increasingly favorable to employers and employees alike, folks can move where they've always wanted to live, not base their housing decision on where the jobs are to be found. Likewise, in my vision, more employers seize opportunities to start companies far away from the metropolises with high costs-of-living, filling our flyover states back up.

I envision a future of the renaissance of small towns and rural areas, as people take advantage of the new reality and make a choice for community. There are disincentives enough to living in large groups these days – wouldn't it be lovely if people saw that they have another choice?

I envision family bonds strengthening as Americans no longer must choose between individual excellence and participation in extended family life. I envision a future where people embrace the diversity of those around them – diversity of talents, diversity of desire, and diversity of what we find meaningful. There is plenty of good and meaningful work to go around, and it is past time that we put the lie that meaning is a luxury that only a few can afford.

It is time to reprioritize. Education may never be the same, so your need to live near a good school district just got tossed in the air. But you have the internet, and the resources of all of history to replace what was.

Jobs may never go back to the way they were – you might find yourself in a new career, you might find yourself in the same career, just in your home office rather than a cubicle. You might find yourself juggling multiple streams of income – but isn't that what they say is the most secure? And did you like your community-killing commute?

As uncertainty increases, your need to trust those around you likewise increases. You might find yourself wanting to move closer to your extended family, or to a smaller community where you know more of the faces around you. You might realize that now is the time to turn those weak bonds in your current social circle into the strong bonds of a functional community ready to have one another's backs. This is the moment of change.

The twentieth century aimed to solve a lot of problems like hunger, sickness, inequity... the motives (at least on their faces) were pure. But also in the twentieth century, humans developed the power to reign in nature herself, to control her. And we called it good. We called white bread good – after all, it was the bread of the rich. We called chemical fertilizers, pesticides and herbicides good – they made farming easier, required fewer hands, and radically increased yields. We called formula good; it freed up mothers. We called increasing city sizes and numbers good – it meant more and more of us were wealthy and had access to all modernity had to offer. We called our decreased obligations to the communities good – it gave opportunity.

But nature was meant for stewardship – not ownership. The straightening of rivers and chemical farm aids created a dead zone. Formula turns out to not be as nutritionally valuable as breast milk, and eating white bread is not much better for you than eating sugar. Increasing city sizes and numbers have created problems with pollution and crime. Industrialization turned workers into machines and gave us repetitive stress injuries and a lack of a feeling of meaning in ones' work.

Humans are part of nature – we are not machines. We need complicated, meandering lives full of relationships with other humans, with access to nature, with work that matters to us, and to food, water and air that are as close to what God created as possible. This is what makes a good life.

It feels so hopeless, sitting here in Laodicea, sitting behind a computer screen, knowing the office awaits. The traffic is just past that plate-glass window, the angry strangers, the endless competition – the rat race. This is reality. The bucolic dream of baskets of berries and strings of onions and holiday gatherings where you belly laugh, where the old mingle with the young and folks learn to care again – that's impossible. Just a dream.

They would have said that about regenerative agriculture, 50 years ago. As the plow created the dust bowl, and the chemicals brought fertility back, our soil was thought forever gone. Nothing we can do to get it back. Nothing we can do to bring life back; we have no choice but to use the chemicals that are killing our farm workers.

They were wrong. Regenerative agriculture builds soil. It adds moisture. It fosters a place where life can take root – and nature was only waiting for an invitation. Interestingly, it is better to steward the land back to health than to simply ignore it. We humans need to be part of the equation. The land needs our love, needs our touch – needs more of us to come back to her, to build her back.

And this is not just a post-millennial hippie pipe dream. Big companies are investing in regenerative agriculture, and Joel Salatin's farming methods are becoming all the rage with the younger generation who are moving back to the land – back to permaculture, back to slower lives and heritage breeds of animals and plants. Non farmers are finding out how tasty nature can be when she is loved, not chained. The soil is being restored ... yes, in little islands for now, but success has been shown. And success builds upon success.

We could likewise look around ourselves, seeing the islands of suspicion and confirmation bias that we have built. We were given the information superhighway, and it turns out that dredging a river to make it go faster creates erosion and damages the ecological stability of the landscape. Pushing humans to see all the people, all the time online is like living in a vast city of strangers who are all yelling, all the time – you never get past that first sentence, and you always feel as if you are under attack. Humans weren't meant for this. We need slower lives, deeper relationships.

But you say – this is impossible. We can't go back. And the view in the rear-view mirror isn't so great – there were a lot of problems. You're right. Just dropping the ball and walking away won't heal us, we have to recreate society intentionally. Carefully. And with love.

1 Corinthians 13: 1-3 If I speak with the tongues of mankind and of angels, but do not have love, I have become a noisy gong or a clanging cymbal. If I have the gift of prophecy and know all mysteries and all knowledge, and if I have all faith so as to remove mountains, but do not have love, I am nothing. And if I give away all my possessions to charity, and if I surrender my body so that I may glory, but do not have love, it does me no good. (NASB)

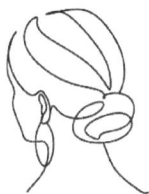 

Goodbye...

Homecoming

"Home is not where you are from, it is where you belong." – Beau Taplin

Come home. Come home to a place where everyone knows your name, where you are loved, needed, and understood. Come home, where you can relax your guard. Come home, where your gifts are appreciated, and in being known, they are put to use. Come home, where you know your neighbors, their stories, their tragedies, and their joys. Come home to a place where you break bread and celebrate together, where you mourn together, where you work together for the common good. Come home to trust.

Imagine holidays filled with celebration, with gatherings, with a pause in everyday life. Just imagine a Thanksgiving where folks stopped to give thanks, with their families, with their communities, with their neighbors. Imagine a Thanksgiving that wasn't overtaken by Christmas, because you weren't so hungry for the Only Real Celebration Allowed that you skipped over a quiet time of reverence.

Imagine celebrating all the disparate holidays on their own terms. Imagine following a liturgical year, with a balance of feasting and fasting, community and introspection. Imagine having others to celebrate with, to make your celebration something other than just a day off, but a day where you did something. Imagine the "no work" of Memorial Day turning into the "yes graveside gathering", and how that might feed your soul's craving for meaning in everyday life, in the cycle of the year, in rhythm.

Imagine a community that celebrated certain holidays – whichever had meaning for them – with greater vivre than the other communities do. Imagine communities being tourists of each other's special days, learning to appreciate one another's art, music, and history. Imagine how that would bind community to community, how much stronger that would make them all.

Imagine, a world where we are so happy in our own homes that we can visit one another, appreciate the differences, and return with our joy and understanding increased. Imagine if we built each other up, stopped to listen and learn, and appreciated without feeling called upon to imitate. Imagine a worldview that embraced difference.

Imagine these things with me. Imagine being part of creating them, recreating them, and having them. Can you imagine such riches? Imagine being part of something where you felt trust, you felt love for the brethren, you felt at home. When was the last time you were home?

We try, in Laodicea, to insist that we can only be home when we are made the same. But that is impossible – we have millennia of different choices behind us that affect our starting points, we have our own passions and choices that have affected the course of our present lives, we have different raw materials, different cultures, different educations, different priorities. Insisting on making us the same is folly.

Just as individuals have their own lives to live, their own goals to pursue and their own families to care for, communities likewise have their own priorities. And each community belongs in a larger community and with a family of smaller communities, whether that be a group of neighborhoods in a big city, or multiple small towns in a county. Then each larger community contributes to the state and the country at larger.

When life is rightly ordered, the individual's first loyalties are to his family and the community in which he lives. These small arenas can reflexively prioritize the welfare of the individual and the family in return.

When our allegiance grows too large, it becomes weak. You don't do great things for those you neither know nor understand, not as a rule. You do great things for what you do understand whether that be a family or a set of values.

There are times and seasons when we must all pull together to land something in the net that the smaller communities simply cannot. A war, a pandemic, some other disaster. But the big net has holes too big to fish for everyday needs. That's why smaller is better for everyday things. And everyday things include the cycle of the year, as we come together and celebrate, we maintain the net. We must look out for one another on the microscale. We have to come home, return to the hearth and maintain it. It is here that change is made.

Civilization starts with home, with hearth, with common joys and common heartaches.

"... a state, which is a community of families and aggregations of families in well-being, for the sake of a perfect and self-sufficient life". -Aristotle

About The Author

Amy Fleming is a writer, speaker, housewife, seamstress, and shuffler of paper. She took her BA in Women's Studies with a minor in Sociology from the University of California at Santa Cruz. **Leaving Laodicea** is her third book.

You can find her at Hearthrose.com.

www.ingramcontent.com/pod-product-compliance
Lightning Source LLC
Chambersburg PA
CBHW031503270326
41930CB00006B/224